I0755089

and portraits, — the whole forming a far more complete, elegant, and cheap edition of the British Poets than has ever appeared before.

The numerous testimonials to the excellence of this series, which the publishers have received, both from the press and the public, in all parts of the country, would seem to indicate that a popular want has been met by this edition, which is universally acknowledged to be the best ever issued, both in point of editorship and mechanical execution.

Notices of the Press.

"We cannot speak too highly in praise of this edition — the only one that deserves the name of 'complete' — of the British Poets." — *Boston Daily Advertiser.*

"We really know nothing more worthy of the cordial support of the American public than the Boston edition of the English Poets." — *New York Times.*

"A fairer printed, a more tasteful, or more valuable set of books, cannot be placed in any library." — *New York Courier and Inquirer.*

"The best, the most permanently valuable, the most convenient, and the cheapest edition of the standard poetical literature of Great Britain ever published." — *Home Journal.*

"We regard it as the most beautiful and convenient library edition of the British Poets yet published." — *Philadelphia Evening Bulletin.*

"We do not know any other edition of the English Poets which combines so much excellence." — *Bibliotheca Sacra.*

"Of the typographical beauty and literary accuracy of this edition, the most flattering things have been said by the most competent authorities, and we have rarely witnessed such complete unanimity among critics as this Boston enterprise has elicited." — *Ballou's Pictorial.*

THE BRITISH ESSAYISTS,

PUBLISHED BY

LITTLE, BROWN AND COMPANY,

110 WASHINGTON STREET, BOSTON.

THE BRITISH ESSAYISTS;

WITH PREFACES, HISTORICAL AND BIOGRAPHICAL,

BY A. CHALMERS, F. S. A.

In 38 vols. 16mo.

TATLER,	ADVENTURER,	MIRROR,
SPECTATOR,	WORLD,	LOUNGER,
GUARDIAN,	CONNOISSEUR,	OBSERVER,
RAMBLER,	IDLER,	LOOKER-ON.
	INDEX.	

THE volumes are the exact size and style of LITTLE, BROWN & Co.'s edition of the "British Poets," and sold at the same price, — seventy-five cents per volume, in cloth.

(For sale also in full calf and half calf binding.)

The want of a neat and uniform edition of these Essays, the productions of the best writers of the English tongue, has long been felt, and the present issue is intended to supply the deficiency.

The volumes are of convenient size, handsomely printed from the last English edition, and the price is such as to recommend them to the favor of the public, and especially of those who are engaged in making selections for school and college libraries.

Notices of the Press.

" These works, the flower of the best English literature for a century, merit a place in every library. They have borne a large office in the culture of mind and style for past generations, and for our elders now upon the stage; and we can wish for those entering active or literary life, access to no purer, or more copious, or more stimulating fountains of thought, sentiment, and motive, than are here." — *North American Review.*

"The judgment of the most competent and respected authority has been passed upon these works, and has decided that they are eminently worthy of being kept in constant use." — *Christian Examiner.*

"The value and popularity of the works included in this series will increase as those who read the English language become cultivated, and wish for compositions of the highest rank. For school and family libraries, these books are just what is needed; they are of convenient size, and attractive outward appearance, — their contents are models of composition, their spirit is liberal and manly, — their tone and influence moral and religious, without cant, or a weakness of any kind." — *Boston Transcript.*

"It is superfluous to praise the Essays, — they are by general consent esteemed models of pure English style, and are full of entertainment, knowledge of the world, and moral instruction, — they will be read with pleasure as long as the English language lives." — *New York Commercial Advertiser.*

"No greater service can be done in the cause of good letters than the extensive dissemination of these standard compositions. They embrace the best models of style in the English language." — *Boston Daily Advertiser.*

"As models of English prose they stand unrivalled, and deserve a place in every library, public or private, but especially in every school and town library in the country." — *Boston Atlas.*

"A series of standard works, the value and popularity of which have only increased with time." — *New York Times.*

"No more desirable edition has ever been published." — *New York Evening Post.*

John Gay

THE POETICAL WORKS OF JOHN GAY.

WITH A LIFE OF THE AUTHOR,

BY DR. JOHNSON.

IN TWO VOLUMES.

VOLUME I.

BOSTON:
LITTLE, BROWN AND COMPANY.
NEW YORK: EVANS AND DICKERSON.
PHILADELPHIA: LIPPINCOTT, GRAMBO AND CO.
M.DCCC.LIV.

RIVERSIDE, CAMBRIDGE:
PRINTED BY H. O. HOUGHTON AND COMPANY.

STEREOTYPED BY STONE AND SMART.

ADVERTISEMENT.

These volumes follow, in most respects, the text of Park, which professes to have been collated with the best editions.

CONTENTS.

VOL. I.

FABLES. PART II.

RURAL SPORTS.

A GEORGIC. IN TWO CANTOS. INSCRIBED TO MR. POPE.

TRIVIA:

OR, THE ART OF WALKING THE STREETS OF LONDON.

IN THREE BOOKS.

THE

LIFE OF JOHN GAY.

BY DR. JOHNSON.

JOHN GAY, descended from an old family that had been long in possession of the manor of Goldworthy,* in Devonshire, was born in 1688, at or near Barnstaple, where he was educated by Mr. Luck, who taught the school of that town with good reputation, and, a little before he retired from it, published a volume of Latin and English verses. Under such a master he was likely to form a taste for poetry. Being born without prospect of hereditary riches, he was sent to London in his youth, and placed apprentice with a silk-mercer.

How long he continued behind the counter, or with what degree of softness and dexterity he received and accommodated the ladies, as he probably took no delight in telling it, is not known. The report is, that he was soon weary of either the restraint or servility of his occupation, and easily persuaded his master to discharge him.

The Duchess of Monmouth, remarkable for in-

* Goldworthy does not appear in the *Villare.—Dr. J.*

flexible perseverance in her demand to be treated as a princess, in 1712 took Gay into her service as secretary: by quitting a shop for such service he might gain leisure, but he certainly advanced little in the boast of independence. Of his leisure he made so good use, that he published next year a poem on 'Rural Sports,' and inscribed it to Mr. Pope, who was then rising fast into reputation. Pope was pleased with the honour; and when he became acquainted with Gay, found such attractions in his manners and conversation, that he seems to have received him into his inmost confidence; and a friendship was formed between them which lasted to their separation by death, without any known abatement on either part. Gay was the general favourite of the whole association of wits; but they regarded him as a playfellow rather than a partner, and treated him with more fondness than respect.

Next year he published 'The Shepherd's Week,' six English pastorals, in which the images are drawn from real life, such as it appears among the rustics in parts of England remote from London. Steele, in some parts of 'The Guardian,' had praised Ambrose Philips, as the pastoral writer that yielded only to Theocritus, Virgil, and Spenser. Pope, who had also published pastorals, not pleased to be overlooked, drew up a comparison of his own compositions with those of Philips, in which he covertly gave himself the preference, while he seemed to disown it. Not content with this, he is supposed to have incited Gay to write 'The Shepherd's Week;' to show, that if it be necessary to copy nature with minuteness, rural life must be exhibited such as grossness and ignorance have made it. So far the plan was reasonable; but the pastorals are introduced by a *proeme,* written with such imitation as they could obtain of obsolete language, and by consequence in a style that was never spoken nor written in any age or in any place.

But the effect of reality and truth became conspicuous, even when the intention was to show them grovelling and degraded. These pastorals became popular, and were read with delight, as just representations of rural manners and occupations, by those who had no interest in the rivalry of the poets, nor knowledge of the critical dispute.

In 1713 he brought a comedy called 'The Wife of Bath' upon the stage, but it received no applause; he printed it, however, and seventeen years after, having altered it, and, as he thought, adapted it more to the public taste, he offered it again to the town; but, though he was flushed with the success of the 'Beggar's Opera,' had the mortification to see it again rejected.

In the last year of Queen Anne's life, Gay was made secretary to the Earl of Clarendon, ambassador to the court of Hanover. This was a station that naturally gave him hopes of kindness from every party; but the Queen's death put an end to her favours, and he had dedicated his 'Shepherd's Week' to Bolingbroke, which Swift considered as the crime that obstructed all kindness from the House of Hanover.

He did not, however, omit to improve the right which his office had given him to the notice of the royal family. On the arrival of the Princess of Wales, he wrote a poem, and obtained so much favour, that both the Prince and Princess went to see his 'What d'ye call it?' a kind of mock-tragedy, in which the images were comic, and the action grave; so that, as Pope relates, Mr. Cromwell, who could not hear what was said, was at a loss how to reconcile the laughter of the audience with the solemnity of the scene.

Of this performance the value certainly is but little; but it was one of the lucky trifles that give pleasure by novelty, and was so much favoured by the audience, that envy appeared against it in the form of criticism; and Griffin, a player, in conjunction with Mr. Theobald, a man afterwards more remarkable, produced a pamphlet called 'The Key to the What d'ye call it?' which, says Gay, 'calls me a blockhead, and Mr. Pope a knave.'

But fortune has always been unconstant. Not long afterwards (1717) he endeavoured to entertain the town with 'Three Hours after Marriage,' a comedy, written, as there is sufficient reason for believing, by the joint assistance of Pope and Arbuthnot. One purpose of it was to bring into contempt Dr. Woodward, the fossilist, a man not really or justly contemptible. It had the fate which such outrages deserve; the scene in which Woodward was directly and apparently ridiculed, by the introduction of a mummy and a crocodile, disgusted the audience, and the performance was driven off the stage with general condemnation.

Gay is represented as a man easily incited to hope, and deeply depressed when his hopes were disappointed. This is not the character of a hero; but it may naturally imply something more generally welcome, a soft and civil companion. Whoever is apt to hope good from others is diligent to please them; but he that believes his powers strong enough to force their own way, commonly tries only to please himself.

He had been simple enough to imagine that those who laughed at the 'What d'ye call it?' would raise the fortune of its author; and, finding nothing done, sunk into dejection. His friends endeavoured to divert him. The Earl of Burlington sent him (1716) into Devonshire; the year after, Mr. Pulteney took him to Aix; and in the following year Lord Harcourt invited him to his seat, where, during his visit, the two rural lovers were killed with lightning, as is particularly told in Pope's Letters.

Being now generally known, he published

(1720) his poems by subscription, with such success, that he raised a thousand pounds; and called his friends to a consultation, what use might be best made of it. Lewis, the steward of Lord Oxford, advised him to intrust it to the funds, and live upon the interest; Arbuthnot bade him to intrust it to Providence, and live upon the principal; Pope directed him, and was seconded by Swift, to purchase an annuity.

Gay in that disastrous year* had a present from young Craggs of some South-Sea stock, and once supposed himself to be master of twenty thousand pounds. His friends persuaded him to sell his share; but he dreamed of dignity and splendour, and could not bear to obstruct his own fortune. He was then importuned to sell as much as would purchase a hundred a-year for life, 'which,' says Fenton, 'will make you sure of a clean shirt and a shoulder of mutton every day.' This counsel was rejected; the profit and principal were lost, and Gay sunk under the calamity so low that his life became in danger.

By the care of his friends, among whom Pope appears to have shown particular tenderness, his health was restored; and, returning to his studies, he wrote a tragedy called 'The Captives,' which he was invited to read before the Princess of Wales. When the hour came, he saw the Princess and

* Spence.

her ladies all in expectation, and advancing with reverence too great for any other attention, stumbled at a stool, and falling forwards, threw down a weighty Japan screen. The Princess started, the ladies screamed, and poor Gay, after all the disturbance, was still to read his play.

The fate of 'The Captives,' which was acted at Drury Lane in 1723–4, I know not;* but he now thought himself in favour, and undertook (1726) to write a volume of Fables for the improvement of the young Duke of Cumberland. For this he is said to have been promised a reward, which he had doubtless magnified with all the wild expectations of indigence and vanity.

Next year the Prince and Princess became King and Queen, and Gay was to be great and happy; but upon the settlement of the household he found himself appointed gentleman usher to the Princess Louisa. By this offer he thought himself insulted, and sent a message to the Queen, that he was too old for the place. There seem to have been many machinations employed afterwards in his favour; and diligent court was paid to Mrs. Howard, afterward Countess of Suffolk, who was much beloved by the King and Queen, to engage her interest for his promotion; but solicitations, verses, and flatteries, were thrown away; the lady heard them, and did nothing.

* It was acted seven nights. The author's third night was by command of their Royal Highnesses.—R.

All the pain which he suffered from the neglect, or, as he perhaps termed it, the ingratitude of the court, may be supposed to have been driven away by the unexampled success of the 'Beggar's Opera.' This play, written in ridicule of the musical Italian drama, was first offered to Cibber and his brethren at Drury Lane, and rejected; it being then carried to Rich, had the effect, as was ludicrously said, of *making* Gay *rich*, and Rich *gay*.

Of this lucky piece, as the reader cannot but wish to know the original and progress, I have inserted the relation which Spence has given in Pope's words.

Dr. Swift had been observing once to Mr. Gay, what an odd pretty sort of a thing a Newgate pastoral might make. Gay was inclined to try at such a thing for some time; but afterwards thought it would be better to write a comedy on the same plan. This was what gave rise to the 'Beggar's Opera.' He began on it; and when first he mentioned it to Swift, the Doctor did not much like the project. As he carried it on, he showed what he wrote to both of us, and we now and then gave a correction, or a word or two of advice; but it was wholly of his own writing. When it was done, neither of us thought it would succeed. We showed it to Congreve; who, after reading it over, said, it would either take greatly, or be damned confoundedly. We were all, at the first night of it, in great uncertainty of the event, till we were very much encouraged by overhearing the Duke of Argyle, who sat in the next box to us, say, 'It will do—it must do! I see it in the eyes of them.' This was a good while before the first act was over, and so gave us ease soon; for that Duke (besides his own good taste) has a particular knack, as any one now living, in discovering the taste of the public. He was quite right in this as usual; the good nature of the audience grew stronger and stronger every act, and ended in a clamour of applause.'

Its reception is thus recorded in the notes to the 'Dunciad:'

'This piece was received with greater applause than was ever known. Besides being acted in London sixty-three days without interruption, and renewed the next season with equal applause, it spread into all the great towns of England; was played in many places to the thirtieth and fortieth time; at Bath and Bristol fifty, &c. It made its progress into Wales, Scotland, and Ireland, where it was performed twenty-four days successively. The ladies carried about with them the favourite songs of it in fans, and houses were furnished with it in screens. The fame of it was not confined to the author only. The person who acted Polly, till then obscure, became all at once the favourite of the town; her pictures were engraved, and sold in great numbers; her life written, books of letters and verses to her published, and pamphlets made even of her sayings and jests. Furthermore, it drove out of England (for that season) the Italian opera, which had carried all before it for ten years.'

Of this performance, when it was printed, the reception was different, according to the different opinion of its readers. Swift commended it for the excellence of its morality, as a piece that 'placed all kinds of vice in the strongest and most odious light;' but others, and among them Dr. Herring, afterwards Archbishop of Canterbury, censured it, as giving encouragement not only to vice but to crimes, by making a highwayman the hero, and dismissing him at last unpunished. It has been even said, that after the exhibition of the 'Beggar's Opera,' the gangs of robbers were evidently multiplied.

Both these decisions are surely exaggerated. The play, like many others, was plainly written only to divert, without any moral purpose, and is therefore not likely to do good; nor can it be conceived, without more speculation than life requires or admits, to be productive of much evil. Highwaymen and house-breakers seldom frequent the playhouse, or mingle in any elegant diversion; nor is it possible for any one to imagine that he may rob with safety, because he sees Mackheath reprieved upon the stage.

This objection, however, or some other rather

political than moral, obtained such prevalence, that when Gay produced a second part under the name of 'Polly,' it was prohibited by the Lord Chamberlain; and he was forced to recompense his repulse by a subscription, which is said to have been so liberally bestowed, that what he called oppression ended in profit. The publication was so much favoured, that though the first part gained him four hundred pounds, near thrice as much was the profit of the second.*

He received yet another recompense for this supposed hardship in the affectionate attention of the Duke and Duchess of Queensberry, into whose house he was taken, and with whom he passed the remaining part of his life. The Duke, considering his want of economy, undertook the management of his money, and gave it to him as he wanted it.† But it is supposed that the discountenance of the court sunk deep into his heart, and gave him more discontent than the applauses or tenderness of his friend could overpower. He soon fell into his old distemper, an habitual colic, and languished, though with many intervals of ease and cheerfulness, till a violent fit at last seized him, and hurried him to the grave, as Arbuthnot reported, with more precipitance than he had ever known. He died on the 4th of December, 1732, and was buried in Westminster Abbey. The letter which

* Spence. † Ibid.

brought an account of his death to Swift was laid by for some days unopened, because when he received it he was impressed with the preconception of some misfortune.

After his death, was published a second volume of 'Fables,' more political than the former. His opera of 'Achilles,' was acted, and the profits were given to two widow sisters, who inherited what he left, as his lawful heirs: for he died without a will, though he had gathered* three thousand pounds. There have appeared, likewise, under his name, a comedy called 'The Distressed Wife,' and 'The Rehearsal at Gotham,' a piece of humour.

The character given him by Pope is this; that 'he was a natural man, without design, who spoke what he thought and just as he thought it;' and that 'he was of a timid temper, and fearful of giving offence to the great:' which caution, however, says Pope, was of no avail.†

As a poet, he cannot be rated very high. He was, as I once heard a female critic remark, 'of a lower order.' He had not in any great degree the *mens divinior*, the dignity of genius. Much however must be allowed to the author of a new species of composition, though it be not of the highest kind. We owe to Gay the ballad opera; a mode of comedy which at first was supposed to

* Spence. † Ibid.

delight only by its novelty, but has now, by the experience of half a century, been found so well accommodated to the disposition of a popular audience, that it is likely to keep long possession of the stage. Whether this new drama was the product of judgment or of luck, the praise of it must be given to the inventor; and there are many writers read with more reverence to whom such merit of originality cannot be attributed.

His first performance, 'The Rural Sports,' is such as was easily planned and executed; it is never contemptible nor ever excellent. 'The Fan' is one of those mythological fictions which antiquity delivers ready to the hand, but which, like other things that lie open to every man's use, are of little value. The attention naturally retires from a new tale of Venus, Diana, and Minerva.

His 'Fables' seem to have been a favourite work; for, having published one volume, he left another behind him. Of this kind of fables, the authors do not appear to have formed any distinct or settled notion. Phædrus evidently confounds them with tales; and Gay both with tales and allegorical prosopopœias. A fable or apologue, such as is now under consideration, seems to be, in its genuine state, a narrative in which beings irrational, and sometimes inanimate, *arbores loquuntur, non tantum feræ*, are, for the purpose of moral instruction, feigned to act and speak with human interests and passions. To this description the compositions of Gay do not always conform. For a fable he gives now and then a tale, or an abstracted allegory; and from some, by whatever name they may be called, it will be difficult to extract any moral principle. They are, however, told with liveliness, the versification is smooth, and the diction, though now and then a little constrained by the measure or the rhyme, is generally happy.

To 'Trivia' may be allowed all that it claims; it is sprightly, various, and pleasant. The subject is of that kind which Gay was by nature qualified to adorn; yet some of his decorations may be justly wished away. An honest blacksmith might have done for Patty what is performed by Vulcan. The appearance of Cloacina is nauseous and superfluous: a shoe-boy could have been produced by the casual cohabition of mere mortals. Horace's rule is broken in both cases: there is no *dignus vindice nodus*, no difficulty that required any supernatural interposition. A patten may be made by the hammer of a mortal; and a bastard may be dropped by a human strumpet. On great occasions, and on small, the mind is repelled by useless and apparent falsehood.

Of his little poems the public judgment seems to be right; they are neither much esteemed nor totally despised. The story of the apparition is borrowed from one of the tales of Poggio. Those that please least are the pieces to which Gulliver gave occasion; for who can much delight in the echo of unnatural fiction?

'Dione' is a counterpart to 'Amynta' and 'Pastor Fido,' and other trifles of the same kind, easily imitated, and unworthy of imitation. What the Italians call comedies from a happy conclusion, Gay calls a tragedy from a mournful event; but the style of the Italians and of Gay is equally tragical. There is something in the poetical Arcadia so remote from known reality and speculative possibility, that we can never support its representation through a long work. A pastoral of a hundred lines may be endured; but who will hear of sheep and goats, and myrtle bowers, and purling rivulets, through five acts? Such scenes please barbarians in the dawn of literature, and children in the dawn of life; but will be for the most part thrown away, as men grow wise, and nations grow learned.

FABLES.

INTRODUCTION.

THE SHEPHERD AND THE PHILOSOPHER.

REMOTE from cities liv'd a Swain,
Unvex'd with all the cares of gain;
His head was silver'd o'er with age,
And long experience made him sage;
In summer's heat and winter's cold
He fed his flock and penn'd the fold:
His hours in cheerful labour flew,
Nor envy nor ambition knew:
His wisdom and his honest fame
Through all the country rais'd his name.
A deep Philosopher (whose rules
Of moral life were drawn from schools)
The Shepherd's homely cottage sought,
And thus explor'd his reach of thought:
'Whence is thy learning? hath thy toil
O'er books consum'd the midnight oil?
Hast thou old Greece and Rome survey'd,
And the vast sense of Plato weigh'd?
Hath Socrates thy soul refin'd,
And hast thou fathom'd Tully's mind?
Or, like the wise Ulysses, thrown,
By various fates, on realms unknown,

Hast thou through many cities stray'd,
Their customs, laws, and manners weigh'd?'
The Shepherd modestly replied,—
'I ne'er the paths of learning tried;
Nor have I roam'd in foreign parts
To read mankind, their laws and arts;
For man is practis'd in disguise,
He cheats the most discerning eyes:
Who by that search shall wiser grow,
When we ourselves can never know?
The little knowledge I have gain'd,
Was all from simple Nature drain'd;
Hence my life's maxims took their rise,
Hence grew my settled hate to vice.
'The daily labours of the bee
Awake my soul to industry:
Who can observe the careful ant,
And not provide for future want?
My dog (the trustiest of his kind)
With gratitude inflames my mind:
I mark his true, his faithful way,
And in my service copy Tray.
In constancy and nuptial love,
I learn my duty from the dove.
The hen, who from the chilly air,
With pious wing, protects her care,
And every fowl that flies at large,
Instructs me in a parent's charge.
'From Nature, too, I take my rule,
To shun contempt and ridicule.

I never, with important air,
In conversation overbear.
Can grave and formal pass for wise,
When men the solemn owl despise?
My tongue within my lips I rein;
For who talks much must talk in vain.
We from the wordy torrent fly:
Who listens to the chattering pye?
Nor would I, with felonious slight,
By stealth invade my neighbour's right.
Rapacious animals we hate:
Kites, hawks, and wolves, deserve their fate.
Do not we just abhorrence find
Against the toad and serpent kind?
But Envy, Calumny, and Spite,
Bear stronger venom in their bite.
Thus every object of creation
Can furnish hints to contemplation;
And from the most minute and mean,
A virtuous mind can morals glean.'
'Thy fame is just, (the Sage replies)
Thy virtue proves thee truly wise.
Pride often guides the author's pen;
Books as affected are as men:
But he who studies Nature's laws,
From certain truth his maxims draws;
And those, without our schools, suffice
To make men moral, good, and wise.

FABLES.

TO HIS ROYAL HIGHNESS

WILLIAM DUKE OF CUMBERLAND.

PART I.

THE LION, TIGER, AND TRAVELLER.

Accept, young Prince! the moral lay,
And in these Tales mankind survey;
With early virtues plant your breast,
The specious arts of vice detest.
  Princes, like beauties, from their youth
Are strangers to the voice of Truth.
Learn to contemn all praise betimes,
For flattery 's the nurse of crimes:
Friendship by sweet reproof is shown;
(A virtue never near a throne)
In courts such freedom must offend;
There none presumes to be a friend.
To those of your exalted station,
Each courtier is a dedication:
Must I, too, flatter like the rest,
And turn my morals to a jest?

The Muse disdains to steal from those
Who thrive in courts by fulsome prose.
But shall I hide your real praise,
Or tell you what a nation says?
They in your infant bosom trace
The virtues of your royal race;
In the fair dawning of your mind
Discern you generous, mild, and kind:
They see you grieve to hear distress,
And pant already to redress.
Go on; the height of good attain,
Nor let a nation hope in vain:
For hence we justly may presage
The virtues of a riper age.
True courage shall your bosom fire,
And future actions own your sire.
Cowards are cruel, but the brave
Love mercy, and delight to save.
A Tiger, roaming for his prey,
Sprung on a Traveller in the way;
The prostrate game a Lion spies,
And on the greedy tyrant flies:
With mingled roar resounds the wood,
Their teeth, their claws, distil with blood;
Till, vanquish'd by the Lion's strength,
The spotted foe extends his length.
The Man besought the shaggy lord,
And on his knees for life implor'd:
His life the generous hero gave.
Together walking to his cave,

The Lion thus bespoke his guest:
'What hardy beast shall dare contest
My matchless strength? you saw the fight,
And must attest my power and right.
Forc'd to forego their native home,
My starving slaves at distance roam.
Within these woods I reign alone;
The boundless forest is my own.
Bears, wolves, and all the savage brood,
Have dy'd the regal den with blood.
These carcasses on either hand,
Those bones that whiten all the land,
My former deeds and triumphs tell,
Beneath these jaws what numbers fell.'
'True, (says the Man) the strength I saw
Might well the brutal nation awe;
But shall a monarch, brave, like you,
Place glory in so false a view?
Robbers invade their neighbour's right:
Be lov'd; let justice bound your might.
Mean are ambitious heroes' boasts
Of wasted lands and slaughter'd hosts.
Pirates their power by murders gain;
Wise kings by love and mercy reign.
To me your clemency hath shown
The virtue worthy of a throne.
Heav'n gives you power above the rest,
Like Heav'n, to succour the distrest.'
'The case is plain, (the monach said)
False glory hath my youth misled;

For beasts of prey, a servile train,
Have been the flatterers of my reign.
You reason well: yet tell me, friend,
Did ever you in courts attend?
For all my fawning rogues agree,
That human heroes rule like me.'

THE SPANIEL AND THE CHAMELEON.

A SPANIEL, bred with all the care
That waits upon a favourite heir,
Ne'er felt correction's rigid hand;
Indulg'd to disobey command,
In pamper'd ease his hours were spent:
He never knew what learning meant.
Such forward airs, so pert, so smart,
Were sure to win his lady's heart:
Each little mischief gain'd him praise;
How pretty were his fawning ways!
  The wind was south, the morning fair,
He ventures forth to take the air:
He ranges all the meadow round,
And rolls upon the softest ground;
When near him a Chameleon seen,
Was scarce distinguish'd from the green.
  'Dear emblem of the flattering host,
What, live with clowns! a genius lost!

To cities and the court repair;
A fortune cannot fail thee there:
Preferment shall thy talents crown;
Believe me, friend; I know the Town.'
'Sir, (says the Sycophant) like you,
Of old, politer life I knew:
Like you, a courtier born and bred,
Kings lean'd their ear to what I said:
My whisper always met success;
The ladies prais'd me for address:
I knew to hit each courtier's passion,
And flatter'd ev'ry vice in fashion:
But Jove, who hates the liar's ways,
At once cut short my prosperous days,
And, sentenc'd to retain my nature,
Transform'd me to this crawling creature.
Doom'd to a life obscure and mean,
I wander in the sylvan scene:
For Jove the heart alone regards;
He punishes what man rewards.
How different is thy case and mine?
With men at least you sup and dine,
While I, condemn'd to thinnest fare,
Like those I flatter'd, feed on air.'

THE

MOTHER, THE NURSE, AND THE FAIRY.

'Give me a son.' The blessing sent,
Were ever parents more content?
How partial are their doating eyes!
No child is half so fair and wise.
  Wak'd to the morning's pleasing care,
The Mother rose and sought her heir.
She saw the Nurse like one possest,
With wringing hands and sobbing breast.
  'Sure some disaster has befell:
Speak, Nurse; I hope the boy is well.'
  'Dear Madam, think not me to blame;
Invisible the Fairy came:
Your precious babe is hence convey'd,
And in the place a changeling laid.
Where are the father's mouth and nose?
The mother's eyes, as black as sloes?
See, here, a shocking awkward creature,
That speaks a fool in every feature.'
  'The woman 's blind, (the Mother cries)
I see wit sparkle in his eyes.'
  'Lord, Madam, what a squinting leer!
No doubt the Fairy hath been here.'
  Just as she spoke, a pigmy sprite
Pops through the keyhole swift as light;

Perch'd on the cradle's top he stands,
And thus her folly reprimands.
'Whence sprung the vain conceited lie,
That we the world with fools supply?
What! give our sprightly race away
For the dull, helpless sons of Clay!
Besides, by partial fondness shown,
Like you we dote upon our own.
Where yet was ever found a Mother
Who'd give her booby for another?
And should we change with human breed,
Well might we pass for fools indeed.'

THE EAGLE AND ASSEMBLY OF ANIMALS.

As Jupiter's all-seeing eye
Survey'd the worlds beneath the sky;
From this small speck of earth were sent
Murmurs and sounds of discontent;
For every thing alive complain'd
That he the hardest life sustain'd.
Jove calls his Eagle. At the word
Before him stands the royal bird.
The bird, obedient, from heaven's height,
Downward directs his rapid flight;
Then cited every living thing
To hear the mandates of his king.

'Ungrateful creatures! whence arise
These murmurs which offend the skies;
Why this disorder? say the cause;
For just are Jove's eternal laws.
Let each his discontent reveal;
To yon sour Dog I first appeal.'
'Hard is my lot, (the Hound replies;)
On what fleet nerves the Greyhound flies!
While I, with weary step and slow,
O'er plains, and vales, and mountains, go.
The morning sees my chase begun,
Nor ends it till the setting sun.'
'When (says the Greyhound) I pursue,
My game is lost, or caught in view;
Beyond my sight the prey 's secure;
The Hound is slow, but always sure;
And had I his sagacious scent,
Jove ne'er had heard my discontent.'
The Lion crav'd the Fox's art;
The Fox the Lion's force and heart:
The Cock implor'd the Pigeon's flight,
Whose wings were rapid, strong, and light;
The Pigeon strength of wing despis'd,
And the Cock's matchless valour priz'd:
The fishes wish'd to graze the plain,
The Beasts to skim beneath the main:
Thus, envious of another's state,
Each blam'd the partial hand of Fate.
The Bird of Heav'n then cried aloud,
'Jove bids disperse the murmuring crowd;

The god rejects your idle prayers.
Would ye, rebellious mutineers!
Entirely change your name and nature,
And be the very envied creature?—
What, silent all, and none consent?
Be happy, then, and learn content;
Nor imitate the restless mind,
And proud ambition, of mankind.'

THE WILD BOAR AND THE RAM.

Against an elm a sheep was tied,
The butcher's knife in blood was dyed;
The patient flock, in silent fright,
From far beheld the horrid sight:
A savage Boar, who near them stood,
Thus mock'd to scorn the fleecy brood.
'All cowards should be serv'd like you.
See, see, your murderer is in view:
With purple hands, and reeking knife,
He strips the skin yet warm with life.
Your quarter'd sires, your bleeding dams,
The dying bleat of harmless lambs,
Call for revenge. O stupid race!
The heart that wants revenge, is base.'
'I grant (an ancient Ram replies)
We bear no terror in our eyes;

Yet think us not of soul so tame,
Which no repeated wrongs inflame;
Insensible of every ill,
Because we want thy tusks to kill.
Know, those who violence pursue,
Give to themselves the vengeance due;
For in these massacres they find
The two chief plagues that waste mankind.
Our skin supplies the wrangling bar,
It wakes their slumbering sons to war;
And well revenge may rest contented,
Since drums and parchment were invented.'

THE MISER AND PLUTUS.

THE wind was high, the window shakes,
With sudden start the Miser wakes;
Along the silent room he stalks,
Looks back, and trembles as he walks.
Each lock and every bolt he tries,
In every creek and corner pries,
Then opes the chest with treasure stor'd,
And stands in rapture o'er his hoard.
But now with sudden qualms possest,
He wrings his hands, he beats his breast;
By conscience stung he wildly stares,
And thus his guilty soul declares:

'Had the deep earth her stores confin'd,
This heart had known sweet peace of mind.
But virtue 's sold. Good gods! what price
Can recompense the pangs of vice!
O bane of good! seducing cheat!
Can man, weak man, thy power defeat?
Gold banish'd honor from the mind,
And only left the name behind;
Gold sow'd the world with every ill;
Gold taught the murderer's sword to kill:
'Twas gold instructed coward hearts
In treachery's more pernicious arts.
Who can recount the mischiefs o'er?
Virtue resides on earth no more!'—
He spoke, and sigh'd. In angry mood,
Plutus, his god, before him stood.
The Miser, trembling, lock'd his chest;
The Vision frown'd, and thus address'd:—
'Whence is this vile ungrateful rant,
Each sordid rascal's daily cant?
Did I, base wretch! corrupt mankind?—
The fault 's in thy rapacious mind.
Because my blessings are abus'd,
Must I be censur'd, curs'd, accus'd?
Ev'n Virtue's self by knaves is made
A cloak to carry on the trade;
And pow'r (when lodg'd in their possession)
Grows tyranny, and rank oppression.
Thus, when the villain crams his chest,
Gold is the canker of the breast;

'Tis avarice, insolence, and pride,
And every shocking vice beside:
But when to virtuous hands 'tis given,
It blesses, like the dews of Heav'n:
Like Heav'n, it hears the orphan's cries,
And wipes the tears from widows' eyes.
Their crimes on gold shall Misers lay,
Who pawn'd their sordid souls for pay?
Let bravos, then, when blood is spilt,
Upbraid the passive soul with guilt.'

THE LION, THE FOX, AND THE GEESE.

A LION, tir'd with state affairs,
Quite sick of pomp, and worn with cares,
Resolv'd (remote from noise and strife)
In peace to pass his latter life.
It was proclaim'd; the day was set;
Behold the general council met.
The Fox was viceroy nam'd. The crowd
To the new regent humbly bow'd.
Wolves, bears, and mighty tigers bend,
And strive who most shall condescend.
He straight assumes a solemn grace,
Collects his wisdom in his face;
The crowd admire his wit, his sense;
Each word hath weight and consequence.

The flatterer all his art displays:
He who hath pow'r is sure of praise.
A Fox stept forth before the rest,
And thus the servile throng addrest:
'How vast his talents, born to rule,
And train'd in Virtue's honest school!
What clemency his temper sways!
How uncorrupt are all his ways!
Beneath his conduct and command
Rapine shall cease to waste the land.
His brain hath stratagem and art;
Prudence and mercy rule his heart.
What blessings must attend the nation
Under this good administration!'
He said. A Goose, who distant stood,
Harangued apart the cackling brood:
'Whene'er I hear a knave commend,
He bids me shun his worthy friend.
What praise! what mighty commendation!
But 'twas a Fox who spoke th' oration.
Foxes this government may prize
As gentle, plentiful, and wise;
If they enjoy the sweets, 'tis plain
We Geese must feel a tyrant reign.
What havoc now shall thin our race,
When every petty clerk in place,
To prove his taste, and seem polite,
Will feed on Geese both noon and night?'

THE LADY AND THE WASP.

WHAT whispers must the beauty bear!
What hourly nonsense haunts her ear!
Where'er her eyes dispense their charms,
Impertinence around her swarms.
Did not the tender nonsense strike,
Contempt and scorn might look dislike;
Forbidding airs might thin the place,
The slightest flap a fly can chase:
But who can drive the numerous breed?
Chase one, another will succeed.
Who knows a fool, must know his brother;
One fop will recommend another:
And with this plague she's rightly curst,
Because she listen'd to the first.
As Doris, at her toilette's duty,
Sate meditating on her beauty,
She now was pensive, now was gay,
And loll'd the sultry hours away.
As thus in indolence she lies,
A giddy Wasp around her flies.
He now advances, now retires,
Now to her neck and cheek aspires.
Her fan in vain defends her charms;
Swift he returns, again alarms;

For by repulse he bolder grew,
Perch'd on her lip, and sipt the dew.
  She frowns; she frets. 'Good gods! (she cries)
Protect me from these teasing flies:
Of all the plagues that Heav'n hath sent,
A Wasp is most impertinent.'
  The hovering insect thus complain'd;
'Am I then slighted, scorn'd, disdain'd?
Can such offence your anger wake?
'Twas beauty caus'd the bold mistake.
Those cherry lips that breathe perfume,
That cheek so ripe with youthful bloom,
Made me with strong desire pursue
The fairest peach that ever grew.'
  'Strike him not, Jenny, (Doris cries,)
Nor murder Wasps like vulgar flies;
For though he's free, (to do him right)
The creature's civil and polite.'
  In ecstasies away he posts;
Where'er he came the favour boasts;
Brags how her sweetest tea he sips,
And shows the sugar on his lips.
  The hint alarm'd the forward crew;
Sure of success, away they flew:
They share the dainties of the day,
Round her with airy music play:
And now they flutter, now they rest,
Now soar again, and skim her breast.
Nor were they banish'd till she found
That Wasps have stings, and felt the wound.

THE BULL AND THE MASTIFF.

Seek you to train your favourite boy?
Each caution, every care employ;
And ere you venture to confide,
Let his preceptor's heart be tried
Weigh well his manners, life, and scope;
On these depends thy future hope.
As on a time, in peaceful reign,
A Bull enjoy'd the flowery plain,
A Mastiff pass'd; inflam'd with ire,
His eyeballs shot indignant fire;
He foam'd, he rag'd with thirst of blood.
Spurning the ground the monarch stood,
And roar'd aloud: 'Suspend the fight;
In a whole skin go sleep to-night;
Or tell me, ere the battle rage,
What wrongs provoke thee to engage?
Is it ambition fires thy breast,
Or avarice, that ne'er can rest?
From these alone unjustly springs
The world-destroying wrath of kings.'
The surly Mastiff thus returns:
'Within my bosom glory burns.
Like heroes of eternal name,
Whom poets sing, I fight for fame.

The butcher's spirit-stirring mind
To daily war my youth inclin'd;
He train'd me to heroic deed,
Taught me to conquer or to bleed.'
  'Curs'd Dog, (the Bull replied,) no more
I wonder at thy thirst of gore;
For thou (beneath a butcher train'd,
Whose hands with cruelty are stain'd,
His daily murders in thy view)
Must, like thy tutor, blood pursue.
Take, then, thy fate.' With goring wound
At once he lifts him from the ground:
Aloft the sprawling hero flies,
Mangled he falls, he howls, and dies.

THE ELEPHANT AND THE BOOKSELLER.

THE man who with undaunted toils
Sails unknown seas to unknown soils,
With various wonders feasts his sight:
What stranger wonders does he write?
We read, and in description view
Creatures which Adam never knew;
For when we risk no contradiction,
It prompts the tongue to deal in fiction.
Those things that startle me or you
I grant are strange; yet may be true.

Who doubts that Elephants are found
For science and for sense renown'd?
Borri records their strength of parts,
Extent of thought, and skill in arts;
How they perform the law's decrees,
And save the state the hangman's fees;
And how by travel understand
The language of another land.
Let those who question this report,
To Pliny's ancient page resort.
How learn'd was that sagacious breed!
Who now (like them) the Greek can read!
As one of these, in days of yore,
Rummag'd a shop of learning o'er,
Not, like our modern dealers, minding
Only the margin's breadth and binding;
A book his curious eye detains,
Where, with exactest care and pains,
Were every beast and bird portray'd,
That e'er the search of man survey'd;
Their natures and their powers were writ
With all the pride of human wit:
The page he with attention spread,
And thus remark'd on what he read.
'Man with strong reason is endow'd,
A beast scarce instinct is allow'd:
But let this author's worth be tried,
'Tis plain that neither was his guide.
Can he discern the different natures,
And weigh the pow'r of other creatures,

Who by the partial work hath shown
He knows so little of his own?
How falsely is the spaniel drawn!
Did man from him first learn to fawn?
A dog proficient in the trade!
He, the chief flatterer Nature made!
Go, Man! the ways of courts discern,
You 'll find a spaniel still might learn.
How can the fox's theft and plunder
Provoke his censure or his wonder?
From courtiers' tricks and lawyers' arts,
The fox might well improve his parts.
The lion, wolf, and tiger's brood,
He curses, for their thirst of blood:
But is not man to man a prey?
Beasts kill for hunger, men for pay.'
  The Bookseller, who heard him speak,
And saw him turn a page of Greek,
Thought, what a genius have I found!
Then thus address'd with bow profound.
  'Learn'd Sir, if you'd employ your pen
Against the senseless sons of men,
Or write the history of Siam,
No man is better pay than I am;
Or, since you 're learn'd in Greek, let 's see
Something against the Trinity.
  When wrinkling with a sneer his trunk,
'Friend, (quoth the Elephant) you 're drunk:
E'en keep your money and be wise;
Leave man on man to criticize:

For that you ne'er can want a pen
Among the senseless sons of men.
They unprovok'd will court the fray;
Envy 's a sharper spur than pay:
No author ever spar'd a brother;
Wits are gamecocks to one another.'

THE PEACOCK, TURKEY, AND GOOSE.

In beauty faults conspicuous grow;
The smallest speck is seen on snow.
As near a barn, by hunger led,
A peacock with the poultry fed,
All view'd him with an envious eye,
And mock'd his gaudy pageantry.
He, conscious of superior merit,
Contemns their base reviling spirit;
His state and dignity assumes,
And to the sun displays his plumes,
Which, like the Heav'n's o'er-arching skies,
Are spangled with a thousand eyes.
The circling rays, and varied light,
At once confound their dazzled sight;
On every tongue detraction burns,
And malice prompts their spleen by turns.
'Mark with what insolence and pride
The creature takes his haughty stride,

(The Turkey cries). Can spleen contain?
Sure never bird was half so vain.
But were intrinsic merit seen,
We Turkeys have the whiter skin.'
From tongue to tongue they caught abuse,
And next was heard the hissing Goose:
'What hideous legs! what filthy claws!
I scorn to censure little flaws:
Then what a horrid squalling throat!
Ev'n owls are frighted at the note.'
'True: those are faults, (the Peacock cries)
My scream, my shanks, you may despise;
But such blind critics rail in vain.
What, overlook my radiant train!
Know, did my legs (your scorn and sport)
The Turkey or the Goose support,
And did ye scream with harsher sound,
Those faults in you had ne'er been found:
To all apparent beauties blind,
Each blemish strikes an envious mind.'
Thus in assemblies have I seen
A nymph of brightest charms and mien
Wake envy in each ugly face,
And buzzing scandal fills the place.

CUPID, HYMEN, AND PLUTUS.

As Cupid in Cythera's grove
Employ'd the lesser powers of Love;
Some shape the bow, or fit the string,
Some give the taper shaft its wing,
Or turn the polish'd quiver's mould,
Or head the darts with temper'd gold.
  Amidst their toil and various care
Thus Hymen, with assuming air,
Address'd the god: 'Thou purblind Chit,
Of awkward and ill-judging wit,
If matches are not better made,
At once I must forswear my trade.
You send me such ill-coupled folks,
That 'tis a shame to sell them yokes.
They squabble for a pin, a feather,
And wonder how they came together.
The husband 's sullen, dogged, shy,
The wife grows flippant in reply:
He loves command and due restriction,
And she as well likes contradiction:
She never slavishly submits;
She 'll have her will, or have her fits.
He this way tugs, she t' other draws;
The man grows jealous, and with cause.

Nothing can save him but divorce;
And here the wife complies of course.'
'When (says the Boy) had I to do
With either your affairs or you?
I never idly spend my darts;
You trade in mercenary hearts.
For settlements the lawyer 's fee'd;
Is my hand witness to the deed?
If they like cat and dog agree,
Go rail at Plutus, not at me.'
Plutus appear'd, and said, 'Tis true,
In marriage gold is all their view;
They seek not beauty, wit, or sense,
And love is seldom the pretence.
All offer incense at my shrine,
And I alone the bargain sign.
How can Belinda blame her fate?
She only ask'd a great estate.
Doris was rich enough, 'tis true;
Her lord must give her title too:
And every man, or rich or poor,
A fortune asks, and asks no more.'
Avarice, whatever shape it bears,
Must still be coupled with its cares.

THE TAME STAG.

As a young Stag the thicket past,
The branches held his antlers fast;
A clown, who saw the captive hung,
Across the horns his halter flung.
  Now safely hamper'd in the cord,
He bore the present to his lord.
His lord was pleas'd, as was the clown,
When he was tip'd with half-a-crown.
The Stag was brought before his wife;
The tender lady begg'd his life:
'How sleek 's the skin! how speck'd like ermine!
Sure never creature was so charming!'
  At first within the yard confin'd,
He flies and hides from all mankind;
Now bolder grown, with fix'd amaze,
And distant awe, presumes to gaze;
Munches the linen on the lines,
And on a hood or apron dines:
He steals my little master's bread,
Follows the servants to be fed:
Nearer and nearer now he stands,
To feel the praise of patting hands;
Examines every fist for meat,
And, though repuls'd, disdains retreat:

Attacks again with levell'd horns,
And man, that was his terror, scorns.
  Such is the country maiden's fright,
When first a Redcoat is in sight;
Behind the door she hides her face,
Next time at distance eyes the lace:
She now can all his terrors stand,
Nor from his squeeze withdraws her hand.
She plays familiar in his arms,
And every soldier hath his charms.
From tent to tent she spreads her flame;
For custom conquers fear and shame.

THE MONKEY

WHO HAD SEEN THE WORLD.

A MONKEY, to reform the times,
Resolv'd to visit foreign climes;
For men in distant regions roam
To bring politer manners home.
So forth he fares, all toil defies:
Misfortune serves to make us wise.
  At length the treacherous snare was laid;
Poor Pug was caught; to Town convey'd;
There sold. (How envied was his doom,
Made captive in a lady's room!)

Proud, as a lover, of his chains,
He day by day her favour gains.
Whene'er the duty of the day
The toilette calls; with mimic play
He twirls her knots, he cracks her fan,
Like any other gentleman.
In visits, too, his parts and wit,
When jests grew dull, were sure to hit.
Proud with applause, he thought his mind
In every courtly art refin'd;
Like Orpheus, burnt with public zeal,
To civilize the Monkey-weal;
So watch'd occasion, broke his chain,
And sought his native woods again.
The hairy sylvans round him press,
Astonish'd at his strut and dress.
Some praise his sleeve, and others glote
Upon his rich embroider'd coat,
His dapper periwig commending,
With the black tail behind depending;
His powder'd back, above, below,
Like hoary frosts, or fleecy snow;
But all, with envy and desire,
His fluttering shoulder-knot admire.
'Hear and improve, (he pertly cries)
I come to make a nation wise.
Weigh your own worth; support your place,
The next in rank to human race.
In cities long I pass'd my days,
Convers'd with men, and learn'd their ways.

Their dress, their courtly manners see;
Reform your state, and copy me.
Seek ye to thrive? in flattery deal;
Your scorn, your hate, with that conceal.
Seem only to regard your friends,
But use them for your private ends.
Stint not to truth the flow of wit;
Be prompt to lie whene'er 'tis fit.
Bend all your force to spatter merit;
Scandal is conversation's spirit.
Boldly to every thing pretend,
And men your talents shall commend.
I knew the great. Observe me right;
So shall you grow, like man, polite.'
He spoke, and bow'd. With muttering jaws
The wondering circle grinn'd applause.
Now, warm'd with malice, envy, spite,
Their most obliging friends they bite;
And, fond to copy human ways,
Practise new mischiefs all their days.
Thus the dull lad, too tall for school,
With travel finishes the fool;
Studious of every coxcomb's airs,
He drinks, games, dresses, whores, and swears
O'erlooks with scorn all virtuous arts,
For vice is fitted to his parts.

THE

PHILOSOPHER AND THE PHEASANTS.

The Sage, awak'd at early day,
Through the deep forest took his way;
Drawn by the music of the groves,
Along the winding gloom he roves:
From tree to tree the warbling throats
Prolong the sweet alternate notes:
But where he past he terror threw,
The song broke short, the warblers flew;
The thrushes chatter'd with affright,
And nightingales abhorr'd his sight;
All animals before him ran,
To shun the hateful sight of man.
'Whence is this dread of every creature?
Fly they our figure or our nature?'
As thus he walk'd in musing thought,
His ear imperfect accents caught;
With cautious step he nearer drew,
By the thick shade conceal'd from view.
High on the branch a Pheasant stood,
Around her all her listening brood;
Proud of the blessings of her nest,
She thus a mother's care express'd.

'No dangers here shall circumvent;
Within the woods enjoy content.
Sooner the hawk or vulture trust
Than man, of animals the worst:
In him ingratitude you find,
A vice peculiar to the kind.
The sheep, whose annual fleece is dy'd
To guard his health, and serve his pride,
Forc'd from his fold and native plain,
Is in the cruel shambles slain.
The swarms who, with industrious skill,
His hives with wax and honey fill,
In vain whole summer days employ'd;
Their stores are sold, the race destroy'd.
What tribute from the goose is paid!
Does not her wing all science aid?
Does it not lovers' hearts explain,
And drudge to raise the merchant's gain?
What now rewards this general use?
He takes the quills, and eats the goose.
Man then avoid, detest his ways,
So safety shall prolong your days.
When services are thus acquitted,
Be sure we Pheasants must be spitted.'

THE PIN AND THE NEEDLE.

A PIN who long had serv'd a beauty,
Proficient in the toilette's duty,
Had form'd her sleeve, confin'd her hair,
Or given her knot a smarter air,
Now nearest to her heart was plac'd,
Now in her manteau's tail disgrac'd;
But could she partial Fortune blame,
Who saw her lovers serv'd the same?
At length from all her honours cast,
Through various turns of life she past;
Now glitter'd on a tailor's arm,
Now kept a beggar's infant warm;
Now rang'd within a miser's coat,
Contributes to his yearly groat;
Now, rais'd again from low approach,
She visits in the doctor's coach:
Here, there, by various fortune tost,
At last in Gresham-hall was lost.
Charm'd with the wonders of the show,
On every side, above, below,
She now of this or that inquires,
What least was understood admires,
'Tis plain, each thing so struck her mind,
Her head 's of virtuoso kind.

'And pray what 's this, and this, dear Sir?'
'A needle,' says the interpreter.
She knew the name; and thus the fool
Address'd her as a tailor's tool.
'A needle with that filthy stone,
Quite idle, all with rust o'ergrown!
You better might employ your parts,
And aid the sempstress in her arts;
But tell me how the friendship grew
Between that paltry flint and you.'
'Friend, (says the Needle) cease to blame;
I follow real worth and fame.
Know'st thou the loadstone's pow'r and art,
That virtue virtues can impart?
Of all his talents I partake,
Who then can such a friend forsake?
'Tis I direct the pilot's hand
To shun the rocks and treacherous sand:
By me the distant world is known,
And either India is our own.
Had I with milliners been bred,
What had I been? the guide of thread;
And drudg'd as vulgar Needles do,
Of no more consequence than you.'

THE SHEPHERD'S DOG AND THE WOLF.

A WOLF, with hunger fierce and bold,
Ravag'd the plains, and thinn'd the fold;
Deep in the wood secure he lay,
The thefts of night regal'd the day.
In vain the shepherd's wakeful care
Had spread the toils, and watch'd the snare;
In vain the dog pursued his pace,
The fleeter robber mock'd the chase.
As Lightfoot rang'd the forest round,
By chance his foe's retreat he found.
'Let us awhile the war suspend,
And reason as from friend to friend.'
'A truce?' replies the Wolf. 'Tis done.
The Dog the parley thus begun.
'How can that strong intrepid mind
Attack a weak defenceless kind?
Those jaws should prey on nobler food,
And drink the boar's and lion's blood.
Great souls with generous pity melt,
Which coward tyrants never felt.
How harmless is our fleecy care!
Be brave, and let thy mercy spare.'
'Friend, (says the Wolf) the matter weigh;
Nature design'd us beasts of prey;

As such, when hunger finds a treat,
'Tis necessary Wolves should eat.
If, mindful of the bleating weal,
Thy bosom burn with real zeal,
Hence, and thy tyrant lord beseech;
To him repeat the moving speech;
A Wolf eats sheep but now and then,
Ten thousands are devour'd by men.
An open foe may prove a curse,
But a pretended friend is worse.'

THE PAINTER

WHO PLEASED NOBODY AND EVERYBODY.

Lest men suspect your tale untrue,
Keep probability in view.
The traveller leaping o'er those bounds,
The credit of his book confounds.
Who with his tongue hath armies routed,
Makes ev'n his real courage doubted.
But flattery never seems absurd;
The flatter'd always take your word:
Impossibilities seem just:
They take the strongest praise on trust.

Hyperboles, though ne'er so great,
Will still come short of self-conceit.
So very like a Painter drew,
That every eye the picture knew;
He hit complexion, feature, air,
So just, the life itself was there.
No flattery with his colours laid,
To bloom restor'd the faded maid;
He gave each muscle all its strength;
The mouth, the chin, the nose's length;
His honest pencil touch'd with truth,
And mark'd the date of age and youth.
He lost his friends, his practice fail'd;
Truth should not always be reveal'd:
In dusty piles his pictures lay,
For no one sent the second pay.
Two bustos, fraught with every grace,
A Venus' and Apollo's face,
He plac'd in view: resolv'd to please,
Whoever sat he drew from these,
From these corrected every feature,
And spirited each awkward creature.
All things were set; the hour was come,
His pallet ready o'er his thumb;
My Lord appear'd; and, seated right,
In proper attitude and light,
The Painter look'd, he sketch'd the piece,
Then dipt his pencil, talk'd of Greece,
Of Titan's tints, of Guido's air;
'Those eyes, my Lord, the spirit there

Might well a Raphael's hand require,
To give them all the native fire;
The features, fraught with sense and wit,
You 'll grant are very hard to hit;
But yet with patience you shall view
As much as paint and art can do.'
  Observe the work. My Lord replied,
'Till now I thought my mouth was wide;
Besides my nose is somewhat long;
Dear Sir, for me, 'tis far too young.'
  'Oh! pardon me, (the artist cried)
In this we Painters must decide.
The piece ev'n common eyes must strike,
I warrant it extremely like.'
  My Lord examin'd it a-new;
No looking-glass seem'd half so true.
  A lady came, with borrow'd grace,
He from his Venus form'd her face.
Her lover prais'd the Painter's art;
So like the picture in his heart!
To every age some charm he lent;
Ev'n beauties were almost content.
  Through all the town his art they prais'd;
His custom grew, his price was rais'd.
Had he the real likeness shown,
Would any man the picture own?
But when thus happily he wrought,
Each found the likeness in his thought.

THE LION AND THE CUB.

How fond are men of rule and place,
Who court it from the mean and base!
These cannot bear an equal nigh,
But from superior merit fly.
They love the cellar's vulgar joke,
And lose their hours in ale and smoke.
There o'er some petty club preside;
So poor, so paltry, is their pride!
Nay, ev'n with fools whole nights will sit,
In hopes to be supreme in wit.
If these can read, to these I write,
To set their worth in truest light.
  A Lion-cub, of sordid mind,
Avoided all the lion kind;
Fond of applause, he sought the feasts
Of vulgar and ignoble beasts;
With asses all his time he spent,
Their club's perpetual president.
He caught their manners, looks, and airs;
An ass in every thing but ears!
If e'er his Highness meant a joke,
They grinn'd applause before he spoke;
But at each word what shouts of praise!
'Good gods! how natural he brays!'

Elate with flattery and conceit,
He seeks his royal sire's retreat;
Forward, and fond to show his parts,
His Highness brays; the Lion starts.
'Puppy! that curs'd vociferation
Betrays thy life and conversation:
Coxcombs, an ever-noisy race,
Are trumpets of their own disgrace.'
'Why so severe? (the Cub replies)
Our senate always held me wise.'
'How weak is pride! (returns the sire)
All fools are vain when fools admire!
But know, what stupid asses prize,
Lions and noble beasts despise.'

THE OLD HEN AND THE COCK.

Restrain your child; you'll soon believe
The text which says we sprung from Eve.
As an old Hen led forth her train,
And seem'd to peck to show the grain,
She rak'd the chaff, she scratch'd the ground,
And glean'd the spacious yard around:
A giddy chick, to try her wings,
On the well's narrow margin springs,

And prone she drops. The mother's breast
All day with sorrow was possest.
  A Cock she met; her son she knew;
And in her heart affection grew.
  'My Son, (says she) I grant your years
Have reach'd beyond a mother's cares.
I see you vigorous, strong, and bold;
I hear with joy your triumphs told.
'Tis not from Cocks thy fate I dread;
But let thy ever-wary tread
Avoid yon well; that fatal place
Is sure perdition to our race.
Print this my counsel on thy breast;
To the just gods I leave the rest.'
  He thank'd her care; yet day by day
His bosom burn'd to disobey,
And every time the well he saw,
Scorn'd in his heart the foolish law:
Near and more near each day he drew,
And long'd to try the dangerous view.
  'Why was this idle charge? (he cries)
Let courage female fears despise.
Or did she doubt my heart was brave,
And therefore this injunction gave?
Or does her harvest store the place
A treasure for her younger race?
And would she thus my search prevent?
I stand resolv'd, and dare th' event.'
  Thus said, he mounts the margin's round,
And pries into the depth profound.

He stretch'd his neck; and from below
With stretching neck advanc'd a foe:
With wrath his ruffled plumes he rears,
The foe with ruffled plumes appears:
Threat answer'd threat; his fury grew;
Headlong to meet the war he flew;
But when the watery death he found,
He thus lamented as he drown'd:
'I ne'er had been in this condition,
But for my mother's prohibition.'

THE RAT-CATCHER AND CATS.

THE rats by night such mischief did,
Betty was every morning chid:
They undermin'd whole sides of bacon,
Her cheese was sapp'd, her tarts were taken;
Her pasties, fenc'd with thickest paste,
Were all demolish'd and laid waste:
She curs'd the Cat for want of duty,
Who left her foes a constant booty.
An engineer, of noted skill,
Engag'd to stop the growing ill.
From room to room he now surveys
Their haunts, their works, their secret ways;

Finds where they 'scape an ambuscade,
And whence the nightly sally 's made.
An envious Cat from place to place,
Unseen, attends his silent pace:
She saw that if his trade went on,
The purring race must be undone;
So secretly removes his baits,
And every stratagem defeats.
Again he sets the poison'd toils,
And Puss again the labour foils.
'What foe, to frustrate my designs,
My schemes thus nightly countermines?
(Incens'd, he cries) this very hour
The wretch shall bleed beneath my power.'
So said, a pondrous trap he brought,
And in the fact poor Puss was caught.
'Smuggler, (says he) thou shalt be made.
A victim to our loss of trade.'
The captive Cat, with piteous mews,
For pardon, life, and freedom sues:
'A sister of the science spare;
One interest is our common care.'
'What insolence! (the Man replied)
Shall Cats with us the game divide?
Were all your interloping band
Extinguish'd, or expell'd the land,
We Rat-catchers might raise our fees,
Sole guardians of a nation's cheese!'
A Cat, who saw the lifted knife,
Thus spoke, and sav'd her sister's life:

'In every age and clime we see
Two of a trade can ne'er agree.
Each hates his neighbour for encroaching;
'Squire stigmatizes 'squire for poaching;
Beauties with beauties are in arms,
And scandal pelts each other's charms;
Kings, too, their neighbour kings dethrone,
In hope to make the world their own:
But let us limit our desires,
Not war like beauties, kings, and 'squires;
For though we both one prey pursue,
There 's game enough for us and you.'

THE GOAT WITHOUT A BEARD.

'Tis certain that the modish passions
Descend among the crowd like fashions.
Excuse me, then, if pride, conceit,
(The manners of the fair and great)
I give to monkeys, asses, dogs,
Fleas, owls, goats, butterflies, and hogs.
I say that these are proud: what then?
I never said they equal men.
A Goat (as vain as Goat can be)
Affected singularity:
Whene'er a thymy bank he found,

He roll'd upon the fragrant ground;
And then with fond attention stood,
Fix'd o'er his image in the flood.
'I hate my frowzy beard, (he cries)
My youth is lost in this disguise.
Did not the females know my vigour,
Well might they loathe this reverend figure.'
Resolv'd to smooth his shaggy face,
He sought the barber of the place.
A flippant monkey, spruce and smart,
Hard by, profess'd the dapper art;
His pole with pewter basons hung,
Black rotten teeth in order strung,
Rang'd cups, that in the window stood,
Lin'd with red rags, to look like blood,
Did well his threefold trade explain,
Who shav'd, drew teeth, and breath'd a vein.
The Goat he welcomes with an air,
And seats him in his wooden chair:
Mouth, nose, and cheek, the lather hides;
Light, smooth, and swift, the razor glides.
'I hope your custom, Sir, (says Pug)
Sure never face was half so smug!'
The Goat, impatient for applause,
Swift to the neighbouring hill withdraws;
The shaggy people grinn'd and star'd:
'Heigh-day! what's here? without a beard!
Say, brother, whence the dire disgrace?
What envious hand hath robb'd your face?'—
When thus the fop with smiles of scorn:

'Are beards by civil nations worn?
Ev'n Muscovites have mow'd their chins.
Shall we, like formal Capuchins,
Stubborn in pride, retain the mode,
And bear about the hairy load?
Whene'er we through the village stray,
Are we not mock'd along the way,
Insulted with loud shouts of scorn,
By boys our beards disgrac'd and torn?'
  'Were you no more with Goats to dwell,
Brother, I grant you reason well;
(Replies a bearded chief.) Beside,
If boys can mortify thy pride,
How wilt thou stand the ridicule
Of our whole flock? Affected fool!
Coxcombs, distinguish'd from the rest,
To all but coxcombs are a jest.'

THE OLD WOMAN AND HER CATS.

Who friendship with a knave hath made,
Is judg'd a partner in the trade.
The matron who conducts abroad
A willing nymph, is thought a bawd;
And if a modest girl is seen
With one who cures a lover's spleen,
We guess her not extremely nice,
And only wish to know her price.

'Tis thus that on the choice of friends
Our good or evil name depends.
  A wrinkled hag, of wicked fame,
Beside a little smoky flame
Sate hovering, pinch'd with age and frost;
Her shrivell'd hands, with veins emboss'd,
Upon her knees her weight sustains,
While palsy shook her crazy brains:
She mumbles forth her backward prayers,
An untam'd scold of four-score years:
About her swarm'd a numerous brood
Of Cats, who lank with hunger mew'd.
  Teas'd with their cries, her choler grew,
And thus she sputter'd, 'Hence, ye crew!
Fool that I was, to entertain
Such imps, such fiends, a hellish train!
Had ye been never hous'd and nurs'd,
I for a witch had ne'er been curs'd.
To you I owe that crowds of boys
Worry me with eternal noise;
Straws laid across my pace retard,
The horseshoe's nail'd (each threshold's guard)
The stunted broom the wenches hide,
For fear that I should up and ride;
They stick with pins my bleeding seat,
And bid me show my secret teat.'
  'To hear you prate would vex a saint;
Who hath most reason of complaint?
(Replies a Cat) Let's come to proof.
Had we ne'er starv'd beneath your roof,

We had, like others of our race,
In credit liv'd as beasts of chase.
'Tis infamy to serve a hag;
Cats are thought imps, her broom a nag!
And boys against our lives combine,
Because, 'tis said, your Cats have nine.'

THE BUTTERFLY AND THE SNAIL.

All upstarts, insolent in place,
Remind us of their vulgar race.
  As in the sunshine of the morn
A Butterfly (but newly born)
Sate proudly perking on a rose,
With pert conceit his bosom glows;
His wings (all glorious to behold)
Bedropt with azure, jet, and gold,
Wide he displays; the spangled dew
Reflects his eyes and various hue,
  His now-forgotten friend, a Snail,
Beneath his house, with slimy trail
Crawls o'er the grass, whom when he spies,
In wrath he to the gard'ner cries,
'What means yon peasant's daily toil,
From choking weeds to rid the soil?
Why wake you to the morning's care?
Why with new arts correct the year?

Why grows the peach with crimson hue?
And why the plumbs inviting blue?
Were they to feast his taste design'd,
That vermin of voracious kind?
Crush then the slow, the pilfering race,
So purge thy garden from disgrace.'
  'What arrogance! (the Snail replied)
How insolent is upstart pride!
Hadst thou not thus, with insult vain,
Provok'd my patience to complain,
I had conceal'd thy meaner birth,
Nor trac'd thee to the scum of earth:
For scarce nine suns have wak'd the hours,
To swell the fruit, and paint the flow'rs,
Since I thy humbler life survey'd,
In base, in sordid guise array'd;
A hideous insect, vile, unclean,
You dragg'd a slow and noisome train;
And from your spider-bowels drew
Foul film, and spun the dirty clue.
I own my humble life, good Friend;
Snail was I born, and Snail shall end.
And what's a Butterfly? at best
He's but a caterpillar drest;
And all thy race (a numerous seed)
Shall prove of caterpillar breed.'

THE SCOLD AND THE PARROT.

The husband thus reprov'd his wife:
'Who deals in slander, lives in strife.
Art thou the herald of disgrace,
Denouncing war to all thy race?
Can nothing quell thy thunder's rage,
Which spares nor friend, nor sex, nor age?
That vixen tongue of yours, my dear,
Alarms our neighbors far and near,
Good gods! 'tis like a rolling river,
That murmuring flows, and flows for ever!
Ne'er tir'd, perpetual discord sowing!
Like fame, it gathers strength by going.'
  Heigh-day! (the flippant tongue replies)
How solemn is the fool! how wise!
Is Nature's choicest gift debarr'd?—
Nay, frown not; for I will be heard.
Women of late are finely ridden,
A Parrot's privilege forbidden!
You praise his talk, his squalling song,
But wives are always in the wrong.'
  Now reputations flew in pieces
Of mothers, daughters, aunts, and nieces:
She ran the Parrot's language o'er,
Bawd, hussy, drunkard, slattern, whore;

On all the sex she vents her fury,
Tries and condemns without a jury.
  At once the torrent of her words
Alarm'd cat, monkey, dogs, and birds:
All join their forces to confound her,
Puss spits, the monkey chatters round her;
The yelping cur her heels assaults;
The Magpie blabs out all her faults;
Poll, in the uproar, from his cage,
With this rebuke outscream'd her rage:
  'A Parrot is for talking priz'd,
But prattling women are despis'd.
She who attacks another's honour,
Draws every living thing upon her.
Think, Madam, when you stretch your lungs,
That all your neighbours too have tongues:
One slander must ten thousand get;
The world with interest pays the debt.'

THE CUR AND THE MASTIFF.

A SNEAKING Cur, the master's spy,
Rewarded for his daily lie,
With secret jealousies and fears
Set all together by the ears.
Poor puss to-day was in disgrace,
Another cat supplied her place;

The hound was beat, the Mastiff chid,
The monkey was the room forbid;
Each to his dearest friend grew shy,
And none could tell the reason why.
  A plan to rob the house was laid:
The thief with love seduc'd the maid,
Cajol'd the Cur, and strok'd his head,
And bought his secrecy with bread:
He next the Mastiff's honour tried,
Whose honest jaws the bribe defied:
He stretch'd his hand to proffer more;
The surly Dog his fingers tore.
  Swift ran the Cur; with indignation
The master took his information.
'Hang him, the villain 's curs'd, he cries;
And round his neck the halter ties.
  The Dog his humble suit preferr'd,
And begg'd in justice to be heard.
The master sat. On either hand
The cited Dogs confronting stand;
The cur the bloody tale relates,
And like a lawyer, aggravates.
  'Judge not unheard, (the Mastiff cried)
But weigh the cause of either side.
Think not that treachery can be just;
Take not informers' words on trust;
They ope their hand to every pay,
And you and me by turns betray.'
  He spoke; and all the truth appear'd:
The Cur was hang'd, the Mastiff clear'd.

THE SICK MAN AND THE ANGEL.

'Is there no hope?' the sick man said.
The silent doctor shook his head,
And took his leave with signs of sorrow,
Despairing of his fee to-morrow.
When thus the Man, with gasping breath;
'I feel the chilling wound of Death.
Since I must bid the world adieu,
Let me my former life review.
I grant my bargains well were made,
But all men overreach in trade;
'Tis self-defence in each profession;
Sure self-defence is no transgression.
The little portion in my hands,
By good security on lands
Is well increas'd. If, unawares,
My justice to myself and heirs
Hath let my debtor rot in jail,
For want of good sufficient bail;
If I by writ, or bond, or deed,
Reduc'd a family to need,
My will hath made the world amends;
My hope on charity depends.
When I am number'd with the dead,
And all my pious gifts are read,

By heav'n and earth 'twill then be known
My charities were amply shown.'
  An Angel came: 'Ah! Friend! (he cried)
No more in flattering hope confide.
Can thy good deeds in former times
Outweigh the balance of thy crimes?
What widow or what orphan prays
To crown thy life with length of days?
A pious action 's in thy power,
Embrace with joy the happy hour.
Now while you draw the vital air,
Prove your intention is sincere:
This instant give a hundred pound;
Your neighbours want, and you abound.'
  'But why such haste, (the sick Man whines)
Who knows as yet what Heav'n designs?
Perhaps I may recover still.
That sum and more are in my will.'
  'Fool, (says the Vision) now 'tis plain
Your life, your soul, your heav'n, was gain.
From every side, with all your might,
You scrap'd, and scrap'd beyond your right;
And after death would fain atone,
By giving what is not your own.'
  'While there is life, there 's hope, (he cried)
Then why such haste?' so groan'd and died.

THE

PERSIAN, THE SUN, AND THE CLOUD.

Is there a bard whom genius fires,
Whose every thought the god inspires?
When Envy reads the nervous lines,
She frets, she rails, she raves, she pines;
Her hissing snakes with venom swell;
She calls her venal train from hell:
The servile fiends her nod obey,
And all Curl's authors are in pay.
Fame calls up Calumny and Spite:
Thus shadow owes its birth to light.
As prostrate to the God of Day,
With heart devout, a Persian lay,
His invocation thus begun:
'Parent of Light! all-seeing Sun!
Prolific beam, whose rays dispense
The various gifts of Providence,
Accept our praise, our daily prayer,
Smile on our fields, and bless the year.'
A Cloud, who mock'd his grateful tongue,
The day with sudden darkness hung;
With pride and envy swell'd, aloud
A voice thus thunder'd from the Cloud:
'Weak is this gaudy god of thine,
Whom I at will forbid to shine.

Shall I not vows nor incense know?—
Where praise is due the praise bestow.'
  With fervent zeal the Persian mov'd,
Thus the proud calumny reprov'd:
'It was that god who claims my pray'r
Who gave thee birth, and rais'd thee there;
When o'er his beams the veil is thrown,
Thy substance is but plainer shown:
A passing gale, a puff of wind,
Dispels thy thickest troops combin'd.'
  The gale arose; the vapour tost
(The sport of winds) in air was lost;
The glorious orb the day refines.
Thus envy breaks, thus merit shines.

THE FOX AT THE POINT OF DEATH.

A Fox, in life's extreme decay,
Weak, sick, and faint, expiring lay;
All appetite had left his maw,
And Age disarm'd his mumbling jaw.
His numerous race around him stand,
To learn their dying sire's command:
He rais'd his head with whining moan,
And thus was heard the feeble tone:
  'Ah! sons! from evil ways depart;
My crimes lie heavy on my heart.

See, see the murder'd geese appear!
Why are those bleeding turkeys there?
Why all around this cackling train,
Who haunt my ears for chicken slain?'
 The hungry Foxes round them star'd,
And for the promis'd feast prepar'd:
 'Where, Sir, is all this dainty cheer?
Nor turkey, goose, nor hen, is here.
These are the phantoms of your brain,
And your sons lick their lips in vain.'
 'O gluttons! (says the drooping sire)
Restrain inordinate desire:
Your liquorish taste you shall deplore,
When peace of conscience is no more.
Does not the hound betray our pace,
And gins and guns destroy our race?
Thieves dread the searching eye of pow'r,
And never feel the quiet hour.
Old age (which few of us shall know)
Now puts a period to my woe.
Would you true happiness attain,
Let honesty your passions rein;
So live in credit and esteem,
And the good name you lost redeem.'
 'The counsel's good, (a Fox replies)
Could we perform what you advise.
Think what our ancestors have done;
A line of thieves from son to son:
To us descends the long disgrace,
And infamy hath mark'd our race.

Though we, like harmless sheep, should feed,
Honest in thought, in word, and deed,
Whatever hen-roost is decreas'd,
We shall be thought to share the feast.
The change shall never be believ'd.
A lost good name is ne'er retriev'd.
'Nay, then, (replies the feeble Fox)
But, hark! I hear a hen that clocks:
Go, but be moderate in your food;
A chicken, too, might do me good.'

THE SETTING-DOG AND THE PARTRIDGE.

The ranging Dog the stubble tries,
And searches every breeze that flies;
The scent grows warm; with cautious fear
He creeps, and points the covey near;
The men, in silence, far behind,
Conscious of game, the net unbind.
A Partridge, with experience wise,
The fraudful preparation spies;
She mocks their toils, alarms her brood,
The covey springs, and seeks the wood;
But ere her certain wing she tries,
Thus to the creeping Spaniel cries:

'Thou fawning slave to man's deceit,
Thou pimp of Luxury, sneaking cheat,
Of thy whole species thou disgrace,
Dogs should disown thee of their race!
For if I judge their native parts,
They're born with honest open hearts;
And, ere they serv'd man's wicked ends,
Were generous foes, or real friends.'
When thus the Dog, with scornful smile:
'Secure of wing thou dar'st revile.
Clowns are to polish'd manners blind;
How ignorant is the rustic mind!
My worth sagacious courtiers see,
And to preferment rise like me.
The thriving pimp, who beauty sets,
Hath oft enhanc'd a nation's debts:
Friend sets his friend, without regard,
And ministers his skill reward:
Thus train'd by man I learnt his ways,
And growing favour feasts my days.'
'I might have guess'd, (the Partridge said)
The place where you were train'd and fed;
Servants are apt, and in a trice
Ape to a hair their masters' vice.
You came from court, you say: Adieu!'
She said, and to the covey flew.

THE UNIVERSAL APPARITION.

A RAKE, by every passion rul'd,
With every vice his youth had cool'd;
Disease his tainted blood assails;
His spirits droop, his vigour fails:
With secret ills at home he pines,
And, like infirm old age, declines.
As, twing'd with pain, he pensive sits,
And raves, and prays, and swears by fits;
A ghastly phantom, lean and wan,
Before him rose, and thus began:
'My name, perhaps, hath reach'd your ear;
Attend, and be advis'd by Care.
Nor love, nor honour, wealth, nor pow'r,
Can give the heart a cheerful hour
When health is lost. Be timely wise:
With health all taste of pleasure flies.'
Thus said, the Phantom disappears,
The wary counsel wak'd his fears:
He now from all excess abstains,
With physic purifies his veins;
And, to procure a sober life,
Resolves to venture on a wife.
But now again the Sprite ascends.
Where'er he walks his ear attends;

Insinuates that beauty 's frail,
That perseverance must prevail;
With jealousies his brain inflames,
And whispers all her lovers' names.
In other hours she represents
His household charge, his annual rents,
Increasing debts, perplexing duns,
And nothing for his younger sons.
 Straight all his thought to gain he turns,
And with the thirst of lucre burns.
But when possess'd of fortune's store,
The Spectre haunts him more and more;
Sets want and misery in view,
Bold thieves and all the murdering crew;
Alarms him with eternal frights,
Infests his dream, or wakes his nights.
How shall he chase this hideous guest?
Power may perhaps protect his rest.
To power he rose. Again the Sprite
Besets him morning, noon, and night;
Talks of Ambition's tottering seat,
How Envy persecutes the great;
Of rival hate, of treacherous friends,
And what disgrace his fall attends.
 The court he quits to fly from Care.
And seeks the peace of rural air:
His groves, his fields, amus'd his hours;
He prun'd his trees, he rais'd his flowers.
But Care again his steps pursues,
Warns him of blasts, of blighting dews,

Of plundering insects, snails, and rains,
And droughts that starv'd the labour'd plains.
Abroad, at home, the Spectre's there;
In vain we seek to fly from Care.
 At length he thus the Ghost addrest:
'Since thou must be my constant guest,
Be kind, and follow me no more;
For Care, by right, should go before.'

THE TWO OWLS AND THE SPARROW.

Two formal Owls together sat,
Conferring thus in solemn chat:
 'How is the modern taste decay'd!
Where's the respect to wisdom paid?
Our worth the Grecian sages knew;
They gave our sires the honour due;
They weigh'd the dignity of fowls,
And pry'd into the depth of Owls.
Athens, the seat of learned fame,
With general voice rever'd our name;
On merit title was conferr'd,
And all ador'd th' Athenian bird.'
 'Brother, you reason well; (replies
The solemn mate, with half-shut eyes)
Right: Athens was the seat of learning,
And truly wisdom is discerning.

Besides, on Pallas' helm we sit,
The type and ornament of wit:
But now, alas! we're quite neglected,
And a pert Sparrow's more respected.'
  A Sparrow, who was lodg'd beside,
O'erhears them soothe each other's pride,
And thus he nimbly vents his heat:
  'Who meets a fool must find conceit.
I grant you were at Athens grac'd,
And on Minerva's helm were plac'd;
But every bird that wings the sky,
Except an Owl, can tell you why.
From hence they taught their schools to know
How false we judge by outward show;
That we should never looks esteem,
Since fools as wise as you might seem.
Would ye contempt and scorn avoid,
Let your vainglory be destroy'd:
Humble your arrogance of thought,
Pursue the ways by Nature taught;
So shall you find delicious fare,
And grateful farmers praise your care;
So shall sleek mice your chase reward,
And no keen cat find more regard.'

THE COURTIER AND PROTEUS.

Whene'er a Courtier's out of place,
The country shelters his disgrace;
Where, doom'd to exercise and health,
His house and gardens own his wealth.
He builds new schemes, in hope to gain
The plunder of another reign;
Like Philip's son, would fain be doing,
And sighs for other realms to ruin.
As one of these (without his wand)
Pensive along the winding strand
Employ'd the solitary hour,
In projects to regain his pow'r,
The waves in spreading circles ran,
Proteus arose, and thus began:
'Came you from court? for in your mien
A self-important air is seen.'
He frankly own'd his friends had trick'd him,
And how he fell his party's victim.
'Know, (says the God) by matchless skill
I change to every shape at will;
But yet I'm told, at court you see
Those who presume to rival me.'

Thus said: a snake, with hideous trail,
Proteus extends his scaly mail.
'Know, (says the Man) though proud in place,
All Courtiers are of reptile race.
Like you, they take that dreadful form,
Bask in the sun, and fly the storm;
With malice hiss, with envy glote,
And for convenience change their coat;
With new-got lustre rear their head,
Though on a dunghill born and bred.'
Sudden the god a lion stands;
He shakes his mane, he spurns the sands;
Now a fierce lynx, with fiery glare,
A wolf, an ass, a fox, a bear.
'Had I ne'er liv'd at court (he cries)
Such transformation might surprise;
But there, in quest of daily game,
Each able Courtier acts the same.
Wolves, lions, lynxes, while in place,
Their friends and fellows are their chase.
They play the bear's and fox's part,
Now rob by force, now steal with art.
They sometimes in the senate bray,
Or chang'd again to beasts of prey,
Down from the lion to the ape,
Practise the frauds of every shape.
So said: upon the god he flies,
In cords the struggling captive ties.
'Now, Proteus! now (to truth compell'd)
Speak, and confess thy art excell'd.

Use strength, surprise, or what you will,
The Courtier finds evasions still;
Not to be bound by any ties,
And never forc'd to leave his lies.

THE MASTIFFS.

THOSE who in quarrels interpose,
Must often wipe a bloody nose.
  A Mastiff, of true English blood,
Lov'd fighting better than his food.
When dogs were snarling for a bone,
He long'd to make the war his own,
And often found (when two contend)
To interpose obtain'd his end;
He gloried in his limping pace;
The scars of honour seam'd his face;
In every limb a gash appears,
And frequent fights retrench'd his ears.
  As on a time he heard from far
Two dogs engag'd in noisy war,
Away he scours, and lays about him,
Resolv'd no fray should be without him.
  Forth from his yard a tanner flies,
And to the bold intruder cries,
  'A cudgel shall correct your manners:
Whence sprung this cursed hate to tanners?

While on my dog you vent your spite,
Sirrah! 'tis me you dare not bite.'
  To see the battle thus perplex'd,
With equal rage a butcher vex'd,
Hoarse-screaming from the circled crowd,
To the curs'd Mastiff cries aloud,
  'Both Hockley-hole and Mary-bone
The combats of my dog have known:
He ne'er, like bullies, coward-hearted,
Attacks in public, to be parted.
Think not, rash fool, to share his fame;
Be his the honour or the shame.'
  Thus said, they swore, and rav'd like thunder,
Then dragg'd their fasten'd dogs asunder;
While clubs and kicks from every side
Rebounded from the Mastiff's hide.
  All reeking now with sweat and blood,
Awhile the parted warriors stood,
Then pour'd upon the meddling foe,
Who, worried, howl'd, and sprawl'd below.
He rose; and limping from the fray,
By both sides mangled, sneak'd away.

THE BARLEY-MOW AND THE DUNGHILL.

How many saucy airs we meet
From Temple Bar to Aldgate Street!
Proud rogues, who shar'd the South-sea prey,
And sprung like mushrooms in a day!
They think it mean to condescend
To know a brother or a friend;
They blush to hear their mother's name,
And by their pride expose their shame.
 As cross his yard, at early day,
A careful farmer took his way,
He stopp'd, and leaning on his fork,
Observ'd the flail's incessant work.
In thought he measur'd all his store,
His geese, his hogs, he number'd o'er;
In fancy weigh'd the fleeces shorn,
And multiplied the next year's corn.
 A Barley-mow, which stood beside,
Thus to its musing master cry'd:
'Say, good Sir, is it fit or right
To treat me with neglect and slight;
Me, who contribute to your cheer,
And raise your mirth with ale and beer?
Why thus insulted, thus disgrac'd,
And that vile Dunghill near me plac'd?

Are those poor sweepings of a groom,
That filthy sight, that nauseous fume,
Meet objects here? command it hence;
A thing so mean must give offence.'
  The humble Dunghill thus replied:
'Thy master hears, and mocks thy pride:
Insult not thus the meek and low:
In me thy benefactor know;
My warm assistance gave thee birth,
Or thou hadst perish'd low in earth;
But upstarts, to support their station,
Cancel at once all obligation.'

PYTHAGORAS AND THE COUNTRYMAN.

Pythag'ras rose at early dawn,
By soaring meditation drawn;
To breathe the fragrance of the day,
Through flowery fields he took his way.
In musing contemplation warm,
His steps misled him to a farm,
Where on a ladder's topmost round
A peasant stood; the hammer's sound
Shook the weak barn. 'Say, Friend, what care
Calls for thy honest labour there?
  The Clown with surly voice replies,
'Vengeance aloud for justice cries.

This kite by daily rapine fed,
My hens' annoy, my turkeys' dread,
At length his forfeit life hath paid;
See on the wall his wings display'd,
Here nail'd, a terror to his kind,
My fowls shall future safety find;
My yard the thriving poultry feed,
And my barns' refuse fat the breed.'
'Friend, (says the Sage) the doom is wise;
For public good the murderer dies:
But if these tyrants of the air
Demand a sentence so severe,
Think how the glutton, man, devours;
What bloody feasts regale his hours!
O impudence of pow'r and might,
Thus to condemn a hawk or kite,
When thou, perhaps, carniv'rous sinner,
Hadst pullets yesterday for dinner!'
'Hold, (cried the Clown, with passion heated)
Shall kites and men alike be treated?
When Heav'n the world with creatures stor'd,
Man was ordain'd their sovereign lord.'
'Thus tyrants boast, (the Sage replied)
Whose murders spring from pow'er and pride.
Own then this manlike kite is slain
Thy greater luxury to sustain;
For "Petty rogues submit to Fate,
That great ones may enjoy their state."[1]

[1] Garth's Dispensary.

THE FARMER'S WIFE AND THE RAVEN.

'Why are those tears? why droops your head?
Is then your other husband dead?
Or does a worse disgrace betide?
Hath no one since his death applied?'
'Alas! you know the cause too well;
The salt is spilt, to me it fell;
Then to contribute to my loss,
My knife and fork were laid across:
On Friday, too! the day I dread!
Would I were safe at home in bed!
Last night (I vow to Heav'n 'tis true)
Bounce from the fire a coffin flew.
Next post some fatal news shall tell:
God send my Cornish friends be well!'
'Unhappy widow, cease thy tears,
Nor feel affliction in thy fears;
Let not thy stomach be suspended;
Eat now, and weep when dinner 's ended;
And when the butler clears the table,
For thy desert, I 'll read my Fable.'
Betwixt her swagging pannier's load
A Farmer's Wife to market rode,
And, jogging on, with thoughtful care,
Summ'd up the profits of her ware·

When, starting from her silver dream,
Thus far and wide was heard her scream:
'That Raven on yon left-hand oak
(Curse on his ill-betiding croak)
Bodes me no good.' No more she said,
When poor blind Ball, with stumbling tread
Fell prone; o'erturn'd the pannier lay,
And her mash'd eggs bestrow'd the way.
She, sprawling in the yellow road,
Rail'd, swore, and curs'd: 'Thou croaking toad,
A murrain take thy whoreson throat!
I knew misfortune in the note.'
'Dame, (quoth the Raven) spare your oaths,
Unclench your fist, and wipe your clothes.
But why on me those curses thrown?
Goody, the fault was all your own;
For had you laid this brittle ware
On Dun, the old sure-footed mare,
Though all the Ravens of the Hundred,
With croaking had your tongue out-thunder'd,
Sure-footed Dun had kept her legs,
And you, good Woman, sav'd your eggs.'

THE TURKEY AND THE ANT.

In other men we faults can spy,
And blame the mote that dims their eye;
Each little speck and blemish find,
To our own stronger errors blind.
  A Turkey, tir'd of common food,
Forsook the barn, and sought the wood;
Behind her ran an infant train,
Collecting here and there a grain.
'Draw near, my Birds! (the mother cries)
This hill delicious fare supplies;
Behold the busy negro race,
See millions blacken all the place!
Fear not; like me with freedom eat;
An Ant is most delightful meat.
How bless'd, how envied, were our life,
Could we but 'scape the poulterer's knife!
But man, curs'd man, on Turkeys preys,
And Christmas shortens all our days.
Sometimes with oysters we combine,
Sometimes assist the savoury chine;
From the low peasant to the lord,
The Turkey smokes on every board.
Sure men for gluttony are curs'd,
Of the seven deadly sins the worst.'
  An Ant, who climb'd beyond his reach,
Thus answer'd from the neighb'ring beech:

'Ere you remark another's sin,
Bid thy own conscience look within;
Control thy more voracious bill,
Nor for a breakfast nations kill.'

THE FATHER AND JUPITER.

The Man to Jove his suit preferr'd;
He begg'd a wife: his prayer was heard.
Jove wonder'd at his bold addressing;
For how precarious is the blessing!
  A wife he takes: and now for heirs
Again he worries Heav'n with prayers.
Jove nods assent: two hopeful boys
And a fine girl reward his joys.
  Now more solicitous he grew,
And set their future lives in view;
He saw that all respect and duty
Were paid to wealth, to power, and beauty.
  'Once more (he cries) accept my prayer;
Make my lov'd progeny thy care:
Let my first hope, my favourite boy,
All Fortune's richest gifts enjoy:
My next with strong ambition fire;
May favour teach him to aspire,
Till he the step of power ascend,
And courtiers to their idol bend.

With every grace, with every charm,
My daughter's perfect features arm.
If Heav'n approve, a Father 's bless'd.'—
Jove smiles, and grants his full request.
  The first, a miser at the heart,
Studious of every griping art,
Heaps hoards on hoards with anxious pain,
And all his life devotes to gain.
He feels no joy, his cares increase,
He neither wakes nor sleeps in peace;
In fancied want (a wretch complete)
He starves, and yet he dares not eat.
The next to sudden honours grew;
The thriving art of courts he knew;
He reach'd the height of power and place,
Then fell the victim of disgrace.
  Beauty with early bloom supplies
His daughters cheek, and points her eyes.
The vain coquette each suit disdains,
And glories in her lovers' pains.
With age she fades, each lover flies;
Contemn'd, forlorn, she pines and dies.
  When Jove the Father's grief survey'd,
And heard him Heav'n and Fate upbraid,
Thus spoke the God: 'By outward show
Men judge of happiness and woe:
Shall ignorance of good and ill
Dare to direct the eternal will?
Seek virtue; and, of that possest,
To Providence resign the rest.'

THE TWO MONKEYS.

The learned, full of inward pride,
The fops of outward show deride;
The fop, with learning at defiance,
Scoffs at the pedant and the science:
The Don, a formal solemn strutter,
Despises Monsieur's airs and flutter;
While Monsieur mocks the formal fool,
Who looks, and speaks, and walks, by rule.
Britain, a medley of the twain,
As pert as France, as grave as Spain,
In fancy wiser than the rest,
Laughs at them both, of both the jest.
Is not the Poet's chiming close
Censur'd by all the sons of Prose?
While bards of quick imagination
Despise the sleepy prose narration.
Men laugh at apes; they men contemn;
For what are we but apes to them?
Two Monkeys went to Southwark fair,
No critics had a sourer air:
They forc'd their way through draggled folks,
Who gap'd to catch Jack Pudding's jokes;
Then took their tickets for the show,
And got by chance the foremost row.

To see their grave observing face,
Provok'd a laugh through all the place.
'Brother, (says Pug, and turn'd his head)
The rabble 's monstrously ill-bred.'
Now through the booth loud hisses ran,
Nor ended till the show began.
The tumbler whirls the flipflap round,
With somersets he shakes the ground;
The cord beneath the dancer springs;
Aloft in air the vaulter swings;
Distorted now, now prone depends,
Now through his twisted arms ascends;
The crowd, in wonder and delight,
With clapping hands applaud the sight.
With smiles, quoth Pug, 'If pranks like these
The giant apes of reason please,
How would they wonder at our arts?
They must adore us for our parts.
High on the twig I 've seen you cling,
Play, twist, and turn in airy ring:
How can those clumsy things like me,
Fly with a bound from tree to tree?
But yet, by this applause, we find
These emulators of our kind
Discern our worth, our parts regard,
Who our mean mimics thus reward.'
'Brother, (the grinning mate replies)
In this I grant that man is wise:
While good example they pursue,
We must allow some praise is due;

But when they strain beyond their guide,
I laugh to scorn the mimic pride;
For how fantastic is the sight,
To meet men always bolt upright,
Because we sometimes walk on two!
I hate the imitating crew.'

THE OWL AND THE FARMER.

An Owl of grave deport and mien,
Who (like the Turk) was seldom seen,
Within a barn had chose his station,
As fit for prey and contemplation:
Upon a beam aloft he sits,
And nods, and seems to think, by fits.
(So have I seen a man of news,
Or Post-boy or Gazette peruse,
Smoke, nod, and talk with voice profound,
And fix the fate of Europe round.)
Sheaves pil'd on sheaves hid all the floor:
At dawn of morn to view his store
The Farmer came. The hooting guest
His self-importance thus exprest:
'Reason in man is mere pretence:
How weak, how shallow, is his sense!
To treat with scorn the Bird of Night,
Declares his folly or his spite.

Then, too, how partial is his praise!
The lark's, the linnet's, chirping lays
To his ill-judging ears are fine,
And nightingales are all divine:
But the more knowing feather'd race
See wisdom stamp'd upon my face.
Whene'er to visit light I deign,
What flocks of fowl compose my train!
Like slaves, they crowd my flight behind,
And own me of superior kind.'
  The farmer laugh'd, and thus replied:
'Thou dull important lump of pride!
Dar'st thou with that harsh grating tongue
Depreciate birds of warbling song?
Indulge thy spleen: know men and fowl
Regard thee, as thou art, an Owl.
Besides, proud Blockhead! be not vain
Of what thou call'st thy slaves and train:
Few follow Wisdom or her rules;
Fools in derision follow fools.'

THE JUGGLERS.

A JUGGLER long through all the Town
Had rais'd his fortune and renown;
You 'd think (so far his art transcends)
The devil at his fingers' ends.

Vice heard his fame, she read his bill;
Convinc'd of his inferior skill,
She sought his booth, and from the crowd
Defied the man of art aloud.
'Is this then he so fam'd for sleight?
Can this slow bungler cheat your sight?
Dares he with me dispute the prize?
I leave it to impartial eyes.'
Provok'd, the Juggler cried, ''Tis done;
In science I submit to none.'
Thus said, the cups and balls he play'd;
By turns this here, that there, convey'd.
The cards, obedient to his words,
Are by a fillip turn'd to birds.
His little boxes change the grain:
Trick after trick deludes the train.
He shakes his bag, he shows all fair:
His fingers spread, and nothing there;
Then bids it rain with showers of gold;
And now his ivory eggs are told;
But when from thence the hen he draws,
Amaz'd spectators hum applause.
Vice now stept forth, and took the place,
With all the forms of his grimace.
'This magic looking-glass, (she cries)
(There, hand it round) will charm your eyes.'
Each eager eye the sight desir'd,
And every man himself admir'd.
Next, to a senator addressing,
'See this bank-note; observe the blessing.

Breathe on the bill. Heigh, pass! 'Tis gone.'
Upon his lips a padlock shown.
A second puff the magic broke;
The padlock vanish'd, and he spoke.
  Twelve bottles rang'd upon the board
All full, with heady liquor stor'd,
By clean conveyance disappear,
And now two bloody swords are there.
  A purse she to a thief expos'd;
At once his ready fingers clos'd.
He opes his fist, the treasure 's fled;
He sees a halter in its stead.
  She bids Ambition hold a wand;
He grasps a hatchet in his hand.
  A box of charity she shows.
Blow here; and a church-warden blows.
'Tis vanish'd with conveyance neat,
And on the table smokes a treat.
  She shakes the dice, the board she knocks,
And from all pockets fills her box.
  She next a meagre rake addrest:
'This picture see; her shape, her breast!
What youth, and what inviting eyes!
Hold her, and have her.' With surprise,
His hand expos'd a box of pills,
And a loud laugh proclaim'd his ills.
A counter, in a miser's hand,
Grew twenty guineas at command:
She bids his heir the sum retain,
And 'tis a counter now again.

A guinea with her touch you see
Take every shape but Charity;
And not one thing you saw, or drew,
But chang'd from what was first in view.
The Juggler now, in grief of heart,
With this submission own'd her art:
'Can I such matchless sleight withstand!
How practice hath improv'd your hand!
But now and then I cheat the throng;
You every day, and all day long.'

THE COUNCIL OF HORSES.

Upon a time a neighing steed,
Who graz'd among a numerous breed,
With mutiny had fir'd the train,
And spread dissension through the plain.
On matters that concern'd the state
The Council met in grand debate.
A Colt, whose eyeballs flam'd with ire,
Elate with strength and youthful fire,
In haste stept forth before the rest,
And thus the listening throng addrest:
'Good gods! how abject is our race,
Condemn'd to slavery and disgrace!
Shall we our servitude retain,
Because our sires have borne the chain?

Consider, friends! your strength and might;
'Tis conquest to assert your right.
How cumbrous is the gilded coach!
The pride of man is our reproach.
Were we design'd for daily toil,
To drag the ploughshare through the soil,
To sweat in harness through the road,
To groan beneath the carrier's load?
How feeble are the two-legg'd kind!
What force is in our nerves combin'd!
Shall then our nobler jaws submit
To foam and champ the galling bit?
Shall haughty man my back bestride?
Shall the sharp spur provoke my side?
Forbid it Heavens! Reject the rein;
Your shame, your infamy, disdain.
Let him the lion first control,
And still the tiger's famish'd growl.
Let us, like them, our freedom claim,
And make him tremble at our name.'
  A general nod approv'd the cause,
And all the circle neigh'd applause.
  When, lo! with grave and solemn pace,
A steed advanc'd before the race,
With age and long experience wise;
Around he cast his thoughtful eyes,
And, to the murmurs of the train,
Thus spoke the Nestor of the plain:
  'When I had health and strength, like you,
The toils of servitude I knew;

Now grateful man rewards my pains,
And gives me all these wide domains.
At will I crop the year's increase;
My latter life is rest and peace.
I grant to man we lend our pains,
And aid him to correct the plains;
But doth not he divide the care,
Through all the labours of the year?
How many thousand structures rise,
To fence us from inclement skies!
For us he bears the sultry day,
And stores up all our winter's hay,
He sows, he reaps the harvest's gain;
We share the toil and share the grain.
Since every creature was decreed
To aid each other's mutual need,
Appease your discontented mind,
And act the part by Heav'n assign'd.'
  The tumult ceas'd. The Colt submitted;
And, like his ancestors, was bitted.

THE HOUND AND THE HUNTSMAN.

Impertinence at first is borne
With heedless slight or smiles of scorn:
Teas'd into wrath, what patience bears
The noisy fool who perseveres?
  The morning wakes, the Huntsman sounds,
At once rush forth the joyful Hounds;
They seek the wood with eager pace,
Through bush, through brier, explore the chase:
Now scatter'd wide they try the plain,
And snuff the dewy turf in vain.
What care, what industry, what pains!
What universal silence reigns!
  Ringwood, a dog of little fame,
Young, pert, and ignorant of game,
At once displays his babbling throat;
The pack, regardless of the note,
Pursue the scent; with louder strain
He still persists to vex the train.
  The Huntsman to the clamour flies,
The smacking lash he smartly plies.
His ribs all welk'd, with howling tone
The puppy thus express'd his moan.
  'I know the music of my tongue
Long since the pack with envy stung.

What will not spite? these bitter smarts
I owe to my superior parts.'
'When Puppies prate, (the Huntsman cried)
They show both ignorance and pride:
Fools may our scorn, not envy, raise,
For envy is a kind of praise.
Had not thy forward noisy tongue
Proclaim'd thee always in the wrong,
Thou might'st have mingled with the rest,
And ne'er thy foolish nose confest:
But fools, to talking ever prone,
Are sure to make their follies known.'

THE POET AND THE ROSE.

I HATE the man who builds his name
On ruins of another's fame:
Thus prudes, by characters o'erthrown,
Imagine that they raise their own;
Thus scribblers covetous of praise,
Think slander can transplant the bays.
Beauties and bards have equal pride,
With both all rivals are decried,
Who praises Lesbia's eyes and feature,
Must call her sister awkward creature;
For the kind flattery's sure to charm,
When we some other nymph disarm.

As in the cool of early day
A Poet sought the sweets of May,
The garden's fragrant breath ascends,
And every stalk with odour bends:
A Rose he pluck'd, he gaz'd, admir'd,
Thus singing, as the Muse inspir'd:—
'Go, Rose, my Chloe's bosom grace;
How happy should I prove,
Might I supply that envied place
With never-fading love!
There, Phœnix-like, beneath her eye,
Involv'd in fragrance, burn and die.
'Know, hapless flower! that thou shalt find
More fragrant Roses there;
I see thy withering head reclin'd
With envy and despair!
One common fate we both must prove;
You die with envy, I with love.'
'Spare your comparisons, (replied
An angry Rose, who grew beside)
Of all mankind you should not flout us;
What can a Poet do without us!
In every love-song Roses bloom;
We lend you colour and perfume:
Does it to Chloe's charms conduce,
To found her praise on our abuse?
Must we, to flatter her, be made,
To wither, envy, pine, and fade?

THE CUR, HORSE, AND SHEPHERD'S DOG.

The lad of all-sufficient merit,
With modesty ne'er damps his spirit;
Presuming on his own deserts,
On all alike his tongue exerts:
His noisy jokes at random throws,
And pertly spatters friends and foes.
In wit and war the bully race
Contribute to their own disgrace:
Too late the forward youth shall find
That jokes are sometimes paid in kind;
Or if they canker in the breast,
He makes a foe who makes a jest.
A village Cur, of snappish race,
The pertest puppy of the place,
Imagin'd that his treble throat
Was blest with Music's sweetest note;
In the mid road he basking lay,
The yelping nuisance of the way;
For not a creature pass'd along
But had a sample of his song.
Soon as the trotting Steed he hears,
He starts, he cocks his dapper ears;
Away he scours, assaults his hoof;
Now near him snarls, now barks aloof;

With shrill impertinence attends,
Nor leaves him till the village ends.
It chanc'd, upon his evil day,
A Pad came pacing down the way;
The Cur, with never-ceasing tongue,
Upon the passing traveller sprung.
The Horse, from scorn provok'd to ire,
Flung backward; rolling in the mire,
The Puppy howl'd, and bleeding lay;
The Pad in peace pursued his way.
  A Shepherd's Dog, who saw the deed,
Detesting the vexatious breed,
Bespoke him thus: 'When coxcombs prate,
They kindle wrath, contempt, or hate;
Thy teasing tongue had judgment tied,
Thou hadst not like a puppy died.'

THE COURT OF DEATH.

Death, on a solemn night of state,
In all his pomp of terror sate:
The attendants of his gloomy reign,
Diseases dire, a ghastly train!
Crowd the vast court. With hollow tone
A voice thus thunder'd from the throne:
'This night our minister we name,
Let every servant speak his claim;

Merit shall bear this ebon wand.'
All, at the word, stretch'd forth their hand.
  Fever, with burning heat possest,
Advanc'd, and for the wand addrest:
'I to the weekly bills appeal,
Let those express my fervent zeal;
On every slight occasion near,
With violence I persevere.'
  Next Gout appears with limping pace,
Pleads how he shifts from place to place;
From head to foot how swift he flies,
And every joint and sinew plies;
Still working when he seems supprest,
A most tenacious stubborn guest.
  A haggard Spectre from the crew
Crawls forth, and thus asserts his due:
''Tis I who taint the sweetest joy,
And in the shape of Love destroy:
My shanks, sunk eyes, and noseless face,
Prove my pretension to the place.'
  Stone urg'd his ever-growing force;
And, next, Consumption's meagre corse,
With feeble voice, that scarce was heard,
Broke with short coughs, his suit preferr'd:
'Let none object my lingering way,
I gain, like Fabius, by delay;
Fatigue and weaken every foe
By long attack, secure, though slow.'
  Plague represents his rapid power,
Who thinn'd a nation in an hour.

All spoke their claim, and hop'd the wand.
Now expectation hush'd the band,
When thus the Monarch from the throne :
'Merit was ever modest known
What, no Physician speak his right !
None here ! but fees their toils requite.
Let then Intemperance take the wand,
Who fills with gold their zealous hand.
You, Fever, Gout, and all the rest,
(Whom wary men, as foes, detest)
Forego your claim ; no more pretend ;
Intemperance is esteem'd a friend ;
He shares their mirth, their social joys,
And as a courted guest destroys :
The charge on him must justly fall,
Who finds employment for you all.'

THE GARDENER AND THE HOG.

A GARD'NER of peculiar taste,
On a young Hog his favour plac'd,
Who fed not with the common herd ;
His tray was to the hall preferr'd :
He wallow'd underneath the board,
Or in his master's chamber snor'd,
Who fondly strok'd him every day,
And taught him all the puppy's play.

Where'er he went, the grunting friend
Ne'er fail'd his pleasure to attend.
  As on a time the loving pair
Walk'd forth to tend the garden's care,
The Master thus address'd the Swine:
  'My house, my garden, all is thine.
On turnips feast whene'er you please,
And riot in my beans and pease,
If the potato's taste delights,
Or the red carrot's sweet invites,
Indulge thy morn and evening hours,
But let due care regard my flow'rs:
My tulips are my garden's pride:
What vast expense those beds supplied!'
  The Hog by chance one morning roam'd,
Where with new ale the vessels foam'd;
He munches now the steaming grains,
Now with full swill the liquor drains.
Intoxicating fumes arise;
He reels, he rolls his winking eyes;
Then staggering through the garden scours,
And treads down painted ranks of flowers:
With delving snout he turns the soil,
And cools his palate with the spoil.
  The Master came, the ruin spied;
'Villain! suspend thy rage, (he cried)
Hast thou, thou most ungrateful sot,
My charge, my only charge, forgot?
What, all my flowers!' no more he said,
But gaz'd, and sigh'd, and hung his head.

The Hog with fluttering speech returns;
'Explain, Sir, why your anger burns.
See there, untouch'd, your tulips strown;
For I devour'd the roots alone.'
At this the Gard'ner's passion grows;
From oaths and threats he fell to blows:
The stubborn brute the blows sustains,
Assaults his leg, and tears the veins.
Ah! foolish Swain! too late you find
That sties were for such friends design'd!
Homeward he limps with painful pace,
Reflecting thus on past disgrace;
'Who cherishes a brutal mate,
Shall mourn the folly soon or late.'

THE MAN AND THE FLEA.

WHETHER on earth, in air, or main,
Sure every thing alive is vain!
Does not the hawk all fowls survey,
As destin'd only for his prey?
And do not tyrants, prouder things,
Think men were born for slaves to kings?
When the crab views the pearly strands,
Or Tagus, bright with golden sands;

Or crawls beside the coral grove,
And hears the ocean roll above;
'Nature is too profuse, (says he)
Who gave all these to pleasure me!'
  When bordering pinks and roses bloom,
And every garden breathes perfume;
When peaches glow with sunny dyes,
Like Laura's cheek when blushes rise;
When the huge figs the branches bend,
When clusters from the vine depend,
The snail looks round on flower and tree,
And cries, 'All these were made for me!'
  'What dignity 's in human nature?'
Says Man, the most conceited creature,
As from a cliff he cast his eye,
And view'd the sea and arched sky.
The sun was sunk beneath the main;
The moon and all the starry train
Hung the vast vault of heav'n: the Man
His contemplation thus began:
  'When I behold this glorious show,
And the wide watery world below,
The scaly people of the main,
The beasts that range the wood or plain,
The wing'd inhabitants of air,
The day, the night, the various year.
And know all these by Heav'n design'd
As gifts to pleasure human-kind,
I cannot raise my worth too high;
Of what vast consequence am I!'

'Not of the importance you suppose,
(Replies a Flea upon his nose:)
Be humble, learn thyself to scan;
Know, pride was never made for man.
'Tis vanity that swells thy mind.
What, Heav'n and earth for thee design'd!
For thee, made only for our need,
That more important Fleas might feed.'

THE HARE AND MANY FRIENDS.

FRIENDSHIP, like love, is but a name,
Unless to one you stint the flame.
The child, whom many fathers share,
Hath seldom known a father's care.
'Tis thus in friendships; who depend
On many, rarely find a friend.
A Hare who, in a civil way,
Complied with every thing, like GAY,
Was known by all the bestial train
Who haunt the wood or graze the plain;
Her care was never to offend,
And every creature was her friend.
As forth she went at early dawn,
To taste the dew-besprinkled lawn,
Behind she hears the hunter's cries,
And from the deep-mouth'd thunder flies:

She starts, she stops, she pants for breath;
She hears the near advance of death;
She doubles to mislead the hound,
And measures back her mazy round,
Till, fainting in the public way,
Half-dead with fear she gasping lay.
What transport in her bosom grew,
When first the Horse appear'd in view!
'Let me, (says she) your back ascend,
And owe my safety to a friend.
You know my feet betray my flight:
To friendship every burden 's light.'
The Horse replied, 'Poor honest puss,
It grieves my heart to see thee thus:
Be comforted, relief is near,
For all your friends are in the rear.'
She next the stately Bull implor'd;
And thus replied the mighty lord:
'Since every beast alive can tell
That I sincerely wish you well,
I may, without offence, pretend
To take the freedom of a friend.
Love calls me hence; a favourite cow
Expects me near yon barley-mow;
And when a lady 's in the case,
You know all other things give place.
To leave you thus might seem unkind,
But see, the Goat is just behind.'
The Goat remark'd her pulse was high,
Her languid head, her heavy eye:

'My back, (says he) may do you harm;
The Sheep's at hand, and wool is warm.'
The Sheep was feeble, and complain'd
His sides a load of wool sustain'd;
Said he was slow; confess'd his fears;
For hounds eat sheep as well as Hares.
She now the trotting Calf address'd,
To save from death a friend distress'd:
'Shall I, (says he) of tender age,
In this important care engage?
Older and abler pass'd you by;
How strong are those! how weak am I!
Should I presume to bear you hence,
Those friends of mine may take offence.
Excuse me, then! you know my heart;
But dearest friends, alas! must part.
How shall we all lament! Adieu;
For see the hounds are just in view.'

FABLES.

PART II.

ADVERTISEMENT.

THESE Fables were finished by Mr. GAY, and intended for the press a short time before his death; when they were left, with his other papers, to the care of his noble friend and patron the Duke of Queensberry; who permitted them to be printed from the originals in the Author's own handwriting.

FABLES.

PART II.

THE DOG AND THE FOX.

TO A LAWYER.

I KNOW you Lawyers can, with ease,
Twist words and meanings as you please;
That language, by your skill made pliant,
Will bend to favor every client;
That 'tis the fee directs the sense,
To make out either side's pretence.
When you peruse the clearest case,
You see it with a double face:
For scepticism is your profession;
You hold there 's doubt in all expression.
  Hence is the bar with fees supplied,
Hence eloquence takes either side.
Your hand would have but paltry gleaning,
Could every man express his meaning.
Who dares presume to pen a deed,
Unless you previously are fee'd?
'Tis drawn; and, to augment the cost,
In dull prolixity engrost.

And now we 're well secur'd by law,
Till the next brother find a flaw.
  Read o'er a will. Was 't ever known
But you could make the will your own?
For when you read, 'tis with intent
To find out meanings never meant.
Since things are thus, *se defendendo*,
I bar fallacious *innuendo*.
  Sagacious Porta's skill could trace
Some beast or bird in every face.
The head, the eye, the nose's shape,
Prov'd this an owl, and that an ape;
When, in the sketches thus design'd,
Resemblance brings some friend to mind,
You show the piece, and give the hint,
And find each feature in the print;
So monstrous-like the portrait 's found,
All know it, and the laugh goes round.
Like him I draw from general nature;
Is 't I or you, then, fix the satire?—
  So, Sir, I beg you spare your pains
In making comments on my strains.
All private slander I detest,
I judge not of my neighbour's breast:
Party and prejudice I hate,
And write no libels on the state.
  Shall not my Fable censure vice,
Because a knave is over nice?
And, lest the guilty hear and dread,
Shall not the decalogue be read?

If I lash vice in general fiction,
Is 't I apply, or self-conviction?
Brutes are my theme: am I to blame,
If men in morals are the same?
I no man call or ape or ass;
'Tis his own conscience holds the glass.
Thus void of all offence I write:
Who claims the fable knows his right.
A shepherd's Dog, unskill'd in sports,
Pick'd up acquaintance of all sorts;
Among the rest a Fox he knew;
By frequent chat their friendship grew.
Says Reynard, 'Tis a cruel case,
That man should stigmatize our race.
No doubt, among us rogues you find,
As among dogs and human kind;
And yet (unknown to me and you)
There may be honest men and true.
Thus slander tries whate'er it can
To put us on the foot with man.
Let my own actions recommend;
No prejudice can blind a friend;
You know me free from all disguise;
My honour as my life I prize.'
By talk like this, from all mistrust
The Dog was cur'd, and thought him just.
As on a time the Fox held forth
On conscience, honesty, and worth,
Sudden he stopp'd; he cock'd his ear;
Low dropt his brushy tail with fear.

'Bless us! the hunters are abroad:
What's all that clatter on the road?
'Hold, (says the Dog) we're safe from harm,
Twas nothing but a false alarm:
At yonder town 'tis market-day;
Some farmer's wife is on the way;
'Tis so, (I know her piebald mare)
Dame Dobbins with her poultry-ware.'
Reynard grew huff. Says he, 'This sneer
From you I little thought to hear;
Your meaning in your looks I see:
Pray what's Dame Dobbins, friend, to me?
Did I e'er make her poultry thinner?
Prove that I owe the dame a dinner.'
'Friend, (quoth the Cur) I meant no harm;
Then why so captious? why so warm?
My words, in common acceptation,
Could never give this provocation.
No lamb (for aught I ever knew)
May be more innocent than you.'
At this, gall'd Reynard winc'd, and swore
Such language ne'er was given before.
'What's lamb to me? this saucy hint
Shows me, base Knave, which way you squint.
If th' other night your master lost
Three lambs, am I to pay the cost?
Your vile reflections would imply
That I'm the thief. You Dog, you lie.'
'Thou knave, thou fool, (the Dog replied)
The name is just, take either side;

Thy guilt these applications speak:
Sirrah, 'tis conscience makes you squeak.'
So saying, on the Fox he flies:
The self-convicted felon dies.

THE VULTURE, THE SPARROW, AND OTHER BIRDS.

TO A FRIEND IN THE COUNTRY.

Ere I begin, I must premise
Our ministers are good and wise;
So, though malicious tongues apply,
Pray what care they, or what care I?
If I am free with courts, be 't known,
I ne'er presume to mean our own.
If general morals seem to joke
On ministers, and such-like folk,
A captious fool may take offence;
What then? He knows his own pretence.
I meddle with no state affairs;
But spare my jest to save my ears.
Our present schemes are too profound,
For Machiavel himself to sound:
To censure 'em I 've no pretension;
I own they 're past my comprehension.
You say, your brother wants a place,
('Tis many a younger brother's case)

And that he very soon intends
To ply the court, and tease his friends.
If there his merits chance to find
A patriot of an open mind,
Whose constant actions prove him just
To both a king's and people's trust,
May he, with gratitude, attend,
And owe his rise to such a friend.
You praise his parts, for business fit,
His learning, probity, and wit;
But those alone will never do,
Unless his patron have 'em too.
I've heard of times (pray God defend us!
We're not so good but he can mend us)
When wicked ministers have trod
On kings and people, law and God;
With arrogance they girt the throne,
And knew no interest but their own.
Then virtue, from preferment barr'd,
Gets nothing but its own reward.
A gang of petty knaves attend 'em,
With proper parts to recommend 'em.
Then if his patron burn with lust,
The first in favour's pimp the first.
His doors are never clos'd to spies,
Who cheer his heart with double lies;
They flatter him, his foes defame,
So lull the pangs of guilt and shame.
If schemes of lucre haunt his brain,
Projectors swell his greedy train:

Vile brokers ply his private ear
With jobs of plunder for the year;
All consciences must bend and ply;
You must vote on and not know why:
Through thick and thin you must go on;
One scruple, and your place is gone.
  Since plagues like these have curs'd a land,
And favourites cannot always stand,
Good courtiers should for change be ready,
And not have principles too steady;
For should a knave engross the pow'r,
(God shield the realm from that sad hour)
He must have rogues or slavish fools;
For what's a knave without his tools?
  Wherever those a people drain,
And strut with infamy and gain,
I envy not their guilt and state,
And scorn to share the public hate.
Let their own servile creatures rise,
By screening fraud and venting lies:
Give me, kind Heav'n, a private station,[1]
A mind serene for contemplation:
Title and profit I resign;
The post of honour shall be mine.
My Fable read, their merits view,
Then herd who will with such a crew.
  In days of yore (my cautious rhymes
Always except the present times)

1 ——When impious men bear sway,
The post of honour is a private station. ADDISON.

A greedy Vulture, skill'd in game,
Inur'd to guilt, unaw'd by shame,
Approach'd the throne in evil hour,
And step by step intrudes to pow'r:
When at the royal Eagle's ear,
He longs to ease the monarch's care.
The monarch grants. With pride elate,
Behold him minister of state!
Around him throng the feather'd rout;
Friends must be serv'd, and some must out;
Each thinks his own the best pretension;
This asks a place, and that a pension.
  The Nightingale was set aside:
A forward Daw his room supplied.
  'This bird (says he) for business fit,
Hath both sagacity and wit:
With all his turns, and shifts, and tricks,
He's docile, and at nothing sticks:
Then with his neighbours one so free
At all times will connive at me.'
  The Hawk had due distinction shown,
For parts and talents like his own.
  Thousands of hireling Cocks attend him,
As blustering bullies to defend him.
  At once the Ravens were discarded,
And Magpies with their posts rewarded,
  Those fowls of omen I detest,
That pry into another's nest.
State lies must lose all good intent,
For they foresee and croak th' event.

My friends ne'er think, but talk by rote,
Speak what they're taught, and so to vote.
'When rogues like these (a Sparrow cries)
To honours and employments rise,
I court no favour, ask no place,
From such preferment is disgrace.
Within my thatch'd retreat I find
(What these ne'er feel) true peace of mind.'

THE BABOON AND THE POULTRY.

TO A LEVEE HUNTER.

We frequently misplace esteem,
By judging men by what they seem.
To birth, wealth, pow'r, we should allow
Precedence, and our lowest bow:
In that is due distinction shown;
Esteem is Virtue's right alone.
With partial eye we're apt to see
The man of noble pedigree:
We're prepossest my Lord inherits,
In some degree, his grandsire's merits;
For those we find upon record,
But find him nothing but my Lord.
When we, with superficial view,
Gaze on the rich, we're dazzled too.
We know that wealth, well understood,
Hath frequent pow'r of doing good,

Then fancy that the thing is done,
As if the pow'r and will were one.
Thus oft the cheated crowd adore
The thriving knaves that keep 'em poor.
The cringing train of pow'r survey;
What creatures are so low as they!
With what obsequiousness they bend!
To what vile actions condescend!
Their rise is on their meanness built,
And flattery is their smallest guilt.
What homage, reverence, adoration,
In every age, in every nation,
Have sycophants to power address'd!
No matter, who the power possess'd.
Let ministers be what they will,
You find their levees always fill:
Ev'n those who have perplex'd a state,
Whose actions claim contempt and hate,
Had wretches to applaud their schemes,
Though more absurd than madmen's dreams.
When barbarous Moloch was invok'd,
The blood of infants only smok'd!
But here (unless all History lies)
Whole realms have been a sacrifice.
Look through all courts: 'tis power we find
The general idol of mankind;
There worshipp'd under every shape:
Alike the lion, fox, and ape,
Are follow'd by time-serving slaves,
Rich prostitutes and needy knaves.

Who then shall glory in his post?
How frail his pride, how vain his boast!
The followers of his prosperous hour
Are as unstable as his power.
Power, by the breath of Flattery nurst,
The more it swells is nearer burst.
The bubble breaks, the gewgaw ends,
And in a dirty tear descends.

Once on a time an ancient maid,
By wishes and by time decay'd,
To cure the pangs of restless thought,
In birds and beasts amusement sought:
Dogs, parrots, apes, her hours employ'd,
With these alone she talk'd and toy'd.

A huge Baboon her fancy took,
(Almost a man in size and look)
He finger'd every thing he found,
And mimic'd all the servants round;
Then, too, his parts and ready wit
Show'd him for every business fit.
With all these talents 'twas but just
That Pug should hold a place of trust;
So to her favourite was assign'd
The charge of all her feather'd kind.
'Twas his to tend 'em eve and morn,
And portion out their daily corn.

Behold him now, with haughty stride,
Assume a ministerial pride.
The morning rose. In hope of picking,
Swans, turkeys, peacocks, ducks, and chicken,

Fowls of all ranks surround his hut,
To worship his important strut.
The minister appears. The crowd,
Now here, now there, obsequious bow'd.
This prais'd his parts, and that his face,
T' other his dignity in place.
From bill to bill the flattery ran:
He hears and bears it like a man;
For when we flatter Self-conceit,
We but his sentiments repeat.
  If we're too scrupulously just,
What profit's in a place of trust?
The common practice of the great
Is to secure a snug retreat:
So Pug began to turn his brain
(Like other folks in place) on gain.
  An apple-woman's stall was near,
Well stock'd with fruits through all the year;
Here every day he cramm'd his guts,
Hence were his hoards of pears and nuts;
For 'twas agreed (in way of trade)
His payments should in corn be made.
  The stock of grain was quickly spent,
And no account which way it went:
Then, too, the Poultry's starv'd condition
Caus'd speculations of suspicion.
The facts were prov'd beyond dispute;
Pug must refund his hoards of fruit;
And, though then minister in chief
Was branded as a public thief.

Disgrac'd, despis'd, confin'd to chains,
He nothing but his pride retains.
  A Goose pass'd by; he knew the face,
Seen every levee while in place.
  'What, no respect! no reverence shown!
How saucy are these creatures grown!
Not two days since (says he) you bow'd
The lowest of my fawning crowd.'
  'Proud fool! (replies the Goose) 'tis true
Thy corn a fluttering levee drew;
For that I join'd the hungry train,
And sold thee flattery for thy grain:
But then, as now, conceited Ape,
We saw thee in thy proper shape.'

THE ANT IN OFFICE.

TO A FRIEND.

You tell me that you apprehend
My verse may touchy folks offend.
In prudence, too, you think my rhymes
Should never squint at courtiers' crimes;
For though nor this nor that is meant,
Can we another's thoughts prevent?
  You ask me, if I ever knew
Court-chaplains thus the lawn pursue?

I meddle not with gown or lawn;
Poets, I grant, to rise must fawn:
They know great ears are over nice,
And never shock their patron's vice.
But I this hackney path despise;
'Tis my ambition not to rise:
If I must prostitute the Muse,
The base conditions I refuse.
  I neither flatter nor defame,
Yet own I would bring guilt to shame.
If I Corruption's hand expose,
I make corrupted men my foes;
What then? I hate the paltry tribe:
Be virtue mine; be theirs the bribe.
I no man's property invade;
Corruption's yet no lawful trade.
Nor would it mighty ills produce,
Could I shame bribery out of use.
I know 't would cramp most politicians,
Were they tied down to these conditions:
'T would stint their power, their riches bound,
And make their parts seem less profound.
Were they denied their proper tools,
How could they lead their knaves and fools?
Were this the case, let's take a view
What dreadful mischiefs would ensue.
Though it might aggrandize the state;
Could private luxury dine on plate?
Kings might indeed their friends reward;
But ministers find less regard.

Informers, sycophants, and spies,
Would not augment the year's supplies.
Perhaps, too, take away this prop,
An annual job or two might drop.
Besides, if pensions were denied,
Could Avarice support its pride?
It might even ministers confound,
And yet the state be safe and sound.
I care not though 'tis understood;
I only mean my country's good:
And (let who will my freedom blame)
I wish all courtiers did the same.
Nay, though some folks the less might get,
I wish the nation out of debt.
I put no private man's ambition
With public good in competition:
Rather than have our laws defac'd,
I'd vote a minister disgrac'd.
I strike at vice, be't where it will;
And what if great folks take it ill?
I hope corruption, bribery, pension,
One may with detestation mention;
Think you the law (let who will take it)
Can *scandalum magnatum* make it;
I vent no slander, owe no grudge,
Nor of another's conscience judge:
At him or him I take no aim,
Yet dare against all vice declaim.
Shall I not censure breach of trust,
Because knaves know themselves unjust?

That steward whose account is clear,
Demands his honour may appear:
His actions never shun the light;
He is, and would be prov'd upright.
But then you think my Fable bears
Allusion too, to state-affairs.
I grant it does: and who's so great,
That has the privilege to cheat?
If then in any future reign
(For ministers may thirst for gain)
Corrupted hands defraud the nation,
I bar no reader's application.
An Ant there was whose forward prate
Controll'd all matters in debate;
Whether he knew the thing or no,
His tongue eternally would go;
For he had impudence at will,
And boasted universal skill,
Ambition was his point in view:
Thus by degrees to power he grew.
Behold him now his drift attain:
He's made chief treasurer of the grain.
But as their ancient laws are just,
And punish breach of public trust,
'Tis order'd (lest wrong application
Should starve that wise industrious nation)
That all accounts be stated clear,
Their stock, and what defray'd the year;
That auditors shall these inspect,
And public rapine thus be check'd.

For this the solemn day was set;
The auditors in council met.
The granary-keeper must explain,
And balance his account of grain.
He brought (since he could not refuse 'em)
Some scraps of paper to amuse 'em.
  An honest Pismire, warm with zeal,
In justice to the public weal,
Thus spoke:—'The nation's hoard is low;
From whence does this profusion flow?
I know our annual funds' amount;
Why such expense? and where's th' account?'
  With wonted arrogance and pride,
The Ant in office thus replied:
'Consider, Sirs, were secrets told,
How could the best-schem'd projects hold?
Should we state-mysteries disclose,
'Twould lay us open to our foes.
My duty and my well-known zeal
Bid me our present schemes conceal:
But, on my honour, all th' expense
(Though vast) was for the swarm's defence.'
  They pass'd th' account as fair and just;
And voted him implicit trust.
  Next year again the granary drain'd,
He thus his innocence maintain'd:
  'Think how our present matters stand,
What dangers threat from every hand;
What hosts of turkeys stroll for food,
No farmer's wife but hath her brood.

Consider when invasion's near,
Intelligence must cost us dear;
And, in this ticklish situation,
A secret told betrays the nation:
But on my honour, all th' expense
(Though vast) was for the swarm's defence.'
  Again, without examination,
They thank'd his sage administration.
  The year revolves. Their treasure spent,
Again in secret service went:
His honour, too, again was pledg'd,
To satisfy the charge alleg'd.
  When thus, with panic shame possess'd,
An auditor his friends address'd:
  'What are we? ministerial tools?
We little knaves are greater fools.
At last this secret is explor'd,
'Tis our corruption thins the hoard.
For every grain we touch'd, at least,
A thousand his own heaps increas'd.
Then for his kin and favourite spies,
A hundred hardly could suffice.
Thus for a paltry sneaking bribe,
We cheat ourselves and all the tribe;
For all the magazine contains
Grows from our annual toil and pains.'
  They vote, th' account shall be inspected;
The cunning plunderer is detected;
The fraud is sentenc'd; and his hoard,
As due, to public use restor'd.

THE BEAR IN A BOAT.

TO A COXCOMB.

THAT man must daily wiser grow,
Whose search is bent himself to know;
Impartially he weighs his scope,
And on firm reason founds his hope;
He tries his strength before the race,
And never seeks his own disgrace;
He knows the compass, sail, and oar,
Or never launches from the shore;
Before he builds, computes the cost,
And in no proud pursuit is lost;
He learns the bounds of human sense,
And safely walks within the fence.
Thus, conscious of his own defect,
Are pride and self-importance check'd.
If then, self-knowledge to pursue,
Direct our life in every view,
Of all the fools that pride can boast,
A Coxcomb claims distinction most.
Coxcombs are of all ranks and kind;
They 're not to sex or age confin'd,
Or rich, or poor, or great, or small,
And vanity besots 'em all.

By ignorance is pride increas'd:
Those most assume who know the least:
Their own false balance gives 'em weight,
But every other finds 'em light.
  Not that all Coxcombs' follies strike,
And draw our ridicule alike;
To different merits each pretends;
This in love-vanity transcends;
That, smitten with his face and shape,
By dress distinguishes the ape;
T' other with learning crams his shelf,
Knows books, and all things but himself.
  All these are fools of low condition,
Compar'd with Coxcombs of ambition:
For those, puff'd up with flattery, dare
Assume a nation's various care.
They ne'er the grossest praise mistrust,
Their sycophants seem hardly just;
For these, in part alone, attest
The flattery their own thoughts suggest.
In this wide sphere a Coxcomb's shown
In other realms besides his own:
The self-deem'd Machiavel at large
By turns controls in every charge.
Does Commerce suffer in her rights?
'Tis he directs the naval flights.
What sailor dares dispute his skill?
He'll be an admiral when he will.
  Now, meddling in the soldiers' trade,
Troops must be hir'd, and levies made:

He gives ambassadòrs their cue,
His cobbled treaties to renew;
And annual taxes must suffice
The current blunders to disguise.
When his crude schemes in air are lost,
And millions scarce defray the cost,
His arrogance (nought undismay'd)
Trusting in self-sufficient aid,
On other rocks misguides the realm,
And thinks a pilot at the helm.
He ne'er suspects his want of skill,
But blunders on from ill to ill;
And when he fails of all intent,
Blames only unforeseen event.
Lest you mistake the application,
The Fable calls me to relation.
  A Bear of shag and manners rough,
At climbing trees expert enough;
For dextrously, and safe from harm,
Year after year he robb'd the swarm:
Thus thriving on industrious toil,
He gloried in his pilfer'd spoil.
  This trick so swell'd him with conceit,
He thought no enterprise too great.
Alike in sciences and arts
He boasted universal parts;
Pragmatic, busy, bustling, bold,
His arrogance was uncontroll'd:
And thus he made his party good,
And grew dictator of the wood.

The beasts, with admiration, stare,
And think him a prodigious Bear.
Were any common booty got,
'Twas his each portion to allot;
For why? he found there might be picking,
Ev'n in the carving of a chicken.
Intruding thus, he by degrees
Claim'd, too, the butcher's larger fees.
And now his overweening pride
In every province will preside.
No task too difficult was found:
His blundering nose misleads the hound,
In stratagem and subtle arts
He overrules the fox's parts.
It chanc'd as, on a certain day,
Along the bank he took his way,
A Boat, with rudder, sail, and oar,
At anchor floated near the shore.
He stopt, and turning to his train,
Thus pertly vents his vaunting strain:
'What blundering puppies are mankind,
In every science always blind!
I mock the pedantry of schools:
What are their compasses and rules?
From me that helm shall conduct learn,
And man his ignorance discern.'
So saying, with audacious pride
He gains the Boat, and climbs the side,
The beasts, astonish'd, line the strand:
The anchor's weigh'd; he drives from land:

The slack sail shifts from side to side ;
The Boat untrimm'd admits the tide.
Borne down, adrift, at random tost,
His oar breaks short, the rudder 's lost.
The Bear, presuming in his skill,
Is here and there officious still;
Till, striking on the dangerous sands,
Aground the shatter'd vessel stands.
To see the bungler thus distrest,
The very fishes sneer and jest:
Ev'n gudgeons join in ridicule,
To mortify the meddling fool.
The clamorous watermen appear,
Threats, curses, oaths, insult his ear :
Seiz'd, thrash'd, and chain'd, he 's dragg'd to land;
Derision shouts along the strand.

THE SQUIRE AND HIS CUR.

TO A COUNTRY GENTLEMAN.

The man of pure and simple heart
Through life disdains a double part;
He never needs the screen of lies,
His inward bosom to disguise:
In vain malicious tongues assail;
Let Envy snarl, let Slander rail,

From Virtue's shield (secure from wound)
Their blunted venom'd shafts rebound.
So shines his light before mankind,
His actions prove his honest mind.
If in his country's cause he rise,
Debating senates to advise,
Unbrib'd, unaw'd, he dares impart
The honest dictates of his heart:
No ministerial frown he fears,
But in his virtue perseveres.
  But would you play the politician,
Whose heart 's averse to intuition,
Your lips at all times, nay, your reason,
Must be controll'd by place and season.
What statesman could his pow'r support,
Were lying tongues forbid the court?
Did princely ears to truth attend,
What minister could gain his end?
How could he raise his tools to place,
And how his honest foes disgrace?
  That politician tops his part,
Who readily can lie with art:
The man 's proficient in his trade;
His power is strong, his fortune 's made:
By that the interest of the throne
Is made subservient to his own:
By that have kings of old, deluded,
All their own friends for his excluded:
By that, his selfish schemes pursuing,
He thrives upon the public ruin.

Antiochus,[1] with hardy pace,
Provok'd the dangers of the chase;
And, lost from all his menial train,
Travers'd the wood and pathless plain.
A cottage lodg'd the royal guest;
The Parthian clown brought forth his best.
The King unknown his feast enjoy'd,
And various chat the hours employ'd.
From wine what sudden friendship springs!
Frankly they talk'd of courts and kings.
'We country-folks (the Clown replies)
Could ope our gracious monarch's eyes.
The King, (as all our neighbours say)
Might he (God bless him!) have his way,
Is sound at heart, and means our good,
And he would do it if he could.
If truth in courts were not forbid,
Nor kings nor subjects would be rid.
Were he in pow'r we need not doubt him;
But that transferr'd to those about him,
On them he throws the regal cares;
And what mind they? Their own affairs.
If such rapacious hands he trust,
The best of men may seem unjust.
From kings to cobblers 'tis the same;
Bad servants wound their master's fame.
In this our neighbours all agree:
Would the King knew as much as we!'

[1] Plutarch.

Here he stopt short. Repose they sought;
The Peasant slept, the Monarch thought.
The courtiers learn'd, at early dawn,
Where their lost sovereign was withdrawn.
The guards' approach our host alarms;
With gaudy coats the cottage swarms.
The crown and purple robes they bring,
And prostrate fall before the King.
The Clown was call'd; the royal guest
By due reward his thanks exprest.
The King then, turning to the crowd,
Who fawningly before him bow'd,
Thus spoke: 'Since, bent on private gain,
Your counsels first misled my reign,
Taught and inform'd by you alone,
No truth my royal ear hath known,
Till here conversing: hence, ye Crew,
For now I know myself and you.'
Whene'er the royal ear's engrost,
State lies but little genius cost:
The favourite then securely robs,
And gleans a nation by his jobs.
Franker and bolder grown in ill,
He daily poisons dares instil;
And, as his present views suggest,
Inflames or soothes the royal breast:
Thus wicked ministers oppress,
When oft the monarch means redress.
Would kings their private subjects hear,
A minister must talk with fear;

If honesty oppos'd his views,
He dar'd not innocence accuse;
'Twould keep him in such narrow bound,
He could not right and wrong confound.
Happy were kings, could they disclose
Their real friends and real foes!
Were both themselves and subjects known,
A monarch's will might be his own.
Had he the use of ears and eyes,
Knaves would no more be counted wise.
But then a minister might lose
(Hard case!) his own ambitious views.
When such as these have vex'd a state,
Pursued by universal hate,
Their false support at once hath fail'd,
And persevering truth prevail'd:
Expos'd, their train of fraud is seen;
Truth will at last remove the screen'

A Country 'Squire, by whim directed,
The true stanch dogs of chase neglected:
Beneath his board no hound was fed;
His hand ne'er strok'd the spaniel's head.
A snappish Cur, alone carest,
By lies had banished all the rest.
Yap had his ear; and defamation
Gave him full scope of conversation.
His sycophants must be preferr'd;
Room must be made for all his herd:
Wherefore, to bring his schemes about,
Old faithful servants all must out.

The Cur on every creature flew,
(As other great men's puppies do)
Unless due court to him were shown,
And both their face and business known:
No honest tongue an audience found;
He worried all the tenants round;
For why? he liv'd in constant fear,
Lest truth by chance should interfere.
If any stranger dar'd intrude,
The noisy Cur his heels pursued.
Now fierce with rage, now struck with dread,
At once he snarled, bit, and fled.
Aloof he bays, with bristling hair,
And thus in secret growls his fear:
'Who knows but Truth, in this disguise,
May frustrate my best-guarded lies?
Should she (thus mask'd) admittance find,
That very hour my ruin 's sign'd.'
Now in his howl's continued sound,
Their words were lost, the voice was drown'd.
Ever in awe of honest tongues,
Thus every day he strain'd his lungs.
It happen'd, in ill-omen'd hour,
That Yap, unmindful of his pow'r,
Forsook his post, to love inclin'd;
A favourite bitch was in the wind.
By her seduc'd, in amorous play,
They frisk'd the joyous hours away:
Thus by untimely love pursuing,
Like Antony he sought his ruin.

For now the 'Squire, unvex'd with noise,
An honest neighbour's chat enjoys:
'Be free, (says he) your mind impart;
I love a friendly open heart.
Methinks my tenants shun my gate;
Why such a stranger grown of late?
Pray tell me what offence they find:
'Tis plain they 're not so well inclin'd.'
'Turn off your Cur, (the Farmer cries)
Who feeds your ear with daily lies.
His snarling insolence offends:
'Tis he that keeps you from your friends.
Were but that saucy puppy checkt,
You 'd find again the same respect.
Hear only him, he 'll swear it too,
That all our hatred is to you:
But learn from us your true estate;
'Tis that curst Cur alone we hate.'
The 'Squire heard Truth. Now Yap rush'd in;
The wide hall echoes with his din:
Yet Truth prevail'd; and, with disgrace,
The dog was cudgell'd out of place.

THE COUNTRYMAN AND JUPITER.

TO MYSELF.

Have you a friend (look round and spy)
So fond, so prepossess'd as I?
Your faults, so obvious to mankind,
My partial eyes could never find.
When, by the breath of Fortune blown,
Your airy castles were o'erthrown,
Have I been ever prone to blame,
Or mortified your hours with shame?
Was I e'er known to damp your spirit,
Or twit you with the want of merit?
'Tis not so strange that Fortune's frown
Still perseveres to keep you down.
Look round, and see what others do.
Would you be rich and honest too?
Have you (like those she rais'd to place)
Been opportunely mean and base?
Have you (as times requir'd) resign'd
Truth, honour, virtue, peace of mind?
If these are scruples, give her o'er;
Write, practise morals, and be poor.
The gifts of Fortune truly rate;
Then, tell me what would mend your state.

If happiness on wealth were built,
Rich rogues might comfort find in guilt.
As grows the miser's hoarded store,
His fears, his wants, increase the more.
Think, GAY, (what ne'er may be the case)
Should Fortune take you into grace,
Would that your happiness augment?
What can she give beyond content?
Suppose yourself a wealthy heir,
With a vast annual income clear!
In all the affluence you possess,
You might not feel one care the less.
Might you not then (like others) find
With change of fortune change of mind?
Perhaps, prófuse beyond all rule,
You might start out a glaring fool;
Your luxury might break all bounds:
Plate, table, horses, stewards, hounds,
Might swell your debts: then, lust of play
No regal income can defray.
Sunk is all credit, writs assail,
And doom your future life to jail.
Or were you dignified with pow'r,
Would that avert one pensive hour?
You might give avarice its swing,
Defraud a nation, blind a king:
Then from the hirelings in your cause,
Though daily fed with false applause,
Could it a real joy impart?—
Great guilt knew never joy at heart.

Is happiness your point in view?
(I mean th' intrinsic and the true)
She nor in camps or courts resides,
Nor in the humble cottage hides;
Yet found alike in every sphere:
Who finds content will find her there.
O'erspent with toil, beneath the shade,
A Peasant rested on his spade:
'Good gods! (he cries) 'tis hard to bear
This load of life from year to year!
Soon as the morning streaks the skies
Industrious labour bids me rise;
With sweat I earn my homely fare,
And every day renews my care.'
Jove heard the discontented strain,
And thus rebuk'd the murmuring swain:
'Speak out your wants, then, honest Friend:
Unjust complaints the gods offend.
If you repine at partial Fate,
Instruct me what could mend your state.
Mankind in every station see.
What wish you? tell me what you 'd be.'
So said, upborne upon a cloud,
The Clown survey'd the anxious crowd.
'Yon face of Care, (says Jove) behold,
His bulky bags are fill'd with gold:
See with what joy he counts it o'er!
That sum to-day hath swell'd his store.'
'Were I that man, (the Peasant cried)
What blessing could I ask beside?'

'Hold, (says the God) first learn to know
True happiness from outward show.
This optic glass of intuition——
Here, take it, view his true condition.'
He look'd, and saw the miser's breast
A troubled ocean, ne'er at rest;
Want ever stares him in the face,
And fear anticipates disgrace:
With conscious guilt he saw him start;
Extortion gnaws his throbbing heart;
And never, or in thought or dream,
His breast admits one happy gleam.
'May Jove, (he cries) reject my pray'r,
And guard my life from guilt and care.
My soul abhors that wretch's fate:
O keep me in my humble state!
But see, amidst a gaudy crowd,
Yon minister so gay and proud;
On him what happiness attends,
Who thus rewards his grateful friends!'
'First take the glass, (the God replies)
Man views the world with partial eyes.'
'Good gods! (exclaims the startled wight)
Defend me from this hideous sight!
Corruption with corrosive smart
Lies cankering on his guilty heart:
I see him with polluted hand
Spread the contagion o'er the land.
Now Avarice with insatiate jaws,
Now Rapine with her harpy claws,

His bosom tears: his conscious breast
Groans with a load of crimes opprest.
See him, mad and drunk with power,
Stand tottering on Ambition's tower.
Sometimes, in speeches vain and proud,
His boasts insult the nether crowd;
Now, seiz'd with giddiness and fear,
He trembles lest his fall is near.
'Was ever wretch like this! (he cries)
Such misery in such disguise!
The change, O Jove! I disavow;
Still be my lot the spade and plough.'
He next, confirm'd by speculation,
Rejects the lawyer's occupation;
For he the statesman seem'd in part,
And bore similitude of heart.
Nor did the soldier's trade inflame
His hopes with thirst of spoil and fame:
The miseries of war he mourn'd;
Whole nations into deserts turn'd.
By these have laws and rights been brav'd;
By these was free-born man enslav'd:
When battles and invasion cease,
Why swarm they in the lands of peace?
'Such change (says he) may I decline;
The scythe and civil arms be mine!'
Thus, weighing life in each condition,
The Clown withdrew his rash petition.
When thus the God: 'How mortals err!
If you true happiness prefer,

'Tis to no rank of life confin'd,
But dwells in every honest mind.
Be justice then your sole pursuit:
Plant virtue, and content 's the fruit.'
  So Jove, to gratify the Clown,
Where first he found him set him down.

THE

MAN, THE CAT, THE DOG, AND THE FLY.

TO MY NATIVE COUNTRY.

Hail, happy land! whose fertile grounds
The liquid fence of Neptune bounds;
By bounteous Nature set apart,
The seat of Industry and Art!
O Britain! chosen port of trade,
May luxury ne'er thy sons invade;
May never minister (intent
His private treasures to augment)
Corrupt thy state. If jealous foes
Thy rights of commerce dare oppose,
Shall not thy fleets their rapine awe?
Who is 't prescribes the ocean law?
  Whenever neighbouring states contend,
'Tis thine to be the general friend.

What is 't who rules in other lands?
On trade alone thy glory stands:
That benefit is unconfin'd,
Diffusing good among mankind:
That first gave lustre to thy reigns,
And scatter'd plenty o'er thy plains:
'Tis that alone thy wealth supplies,
And draws all Europe's envious eyes.
Be commerce, then, thy sole design;
Keep that, and all the world is thine.
When naval traffic ploughs the main,
Who shares not in the merchant's gain?
'Tis that supports the regal state,
And makes the farmer's heart elate:
The numerous flocks that clothe the land
Can scarce supply the loom's demand;
Prolific culture glads the fields,
And the bare heath a harvest yields.
Nature expects mankind should share
The duties of the public care.
Who 's born for sloth?[1] To some we find
The ploughshare's annual toil assign'd:
Some at the sounding anvil glow;
Some the swift-sliding shuttle throw;
Some, studious of the wind and tide,
From pole to pole our commerce guide:
Some (taught by industry) impart
With hands and feet the works of art;

[1] Barrow.

While some, of genius more refin'd,
With head and tongue assist mankind;
Each aiming at one common end,
Proves to the whole a needful friend.
Thus, born each other's useful aid,
By turns are obligations paid.
  The monarch, when his table 's spread,
Is to the clown oblig'd for bread;
And when in all his glory drest,
Owes to the loom his royal vest.
Do not the mason's toil and care
Protect him from th' inclement air?
Does not the cutler's art supply
The ornament that guards his thigh?
All these, in duty to the throne,
Their common obligations own.
'Tis he (his own and people's cause)
Protects their properties and laws:
Thus they their honest toil employ,
And with content the fruits enjoy.
In every rank, or great or small,
'Tis industry supports us all.
  The animals, by want oppress'd,
To man their services address'd:
While each pursued their selfish good,
They hunger'd for precarious food:
Their hours with anxious cares were vext;
One day they fed, and starv'd the next:
They saw that plenty, sure and rife,
Was found alone in social life;

That mutual industry profess'd,
The various wants of man redress'd.
 The Cat, half famish'd, lean and weak,
Demands the privilege to speak.
 'Well, Puss, (says Man) and what can you
To benefit the public do?'
 The Cat replies: 'These teeth, these claws,
With vigilance shall serve the cause
The mouse, destroy'd by my pursuit,
No longer shall your feasts pollute;
Nor rats, from nightly ambuscade,
With wasteful teeth your stores invade.'
 'I grant (says Man) to general use
Your parts and talents may conduce;
For rats and mice purloin our grain,
And threshers whirl the flail in vain:
Thus shall the Cat, a foe to spoil,
Protect the farmer's honest toil.'
 Then turning to the Dog, he cried,
'Well, Sir, be next your merits tried.'
 'Sir, (says the Dog) by self-applause
We seem to own a friendless cause.
Ask those who know me, if distrust
E'er found me treacherous or unjust?
Did I e'er faith or friendship break?
Ask all those creatures; let them speak.
My vigilance and trusty zeal
Perhaps might serve the public weal.
Might not your flocks in safety feed,
Were I to guard the fleecy breed?

Did I the nightly watches keep,
Could thieves invade you while you sleep?'
  The Man replies: ''Tis just and right;
Rewards such service should requite.
So rare, in property, we find
Trust uncorrupt among mankind,
That taken in a public view,
The first distinction is your due.
Such merits all reward transcend:
Be then my comrade and my friend.'
  Addressing now the Fly: 'From you
What public service can accrue?'
'From me! (the fluttering insect said)
I thought you knew me better bred.
Sir, I'm a gentleman: Is't fit
That I to industry submit?
Let mean mechanics, to be fed
By business earn ignoble bread:
Lost in excess of daily joys,
No thought, no care, my life annoys
At noon (the lady's matin hour)
I sip the tea's delicious flower;
On cates luxuriously I dine,
And drink the fragrance of the vine:
Studious of elegance and ease,
Myself alone I seek to please.'
  The Man his pert conceit derides,
And thus the useless coxcomb chides:
  'Hence, from that peach, that downy seat;
No idle fool deserves to eat.

Could you have sapp'd the blushing rind,
And on that pulp ambrosial din'd,
Had not some hand, with skill and toil,
To raise the tree prepar'd the soil?
Consider, sot, what would ensue,
Were all such worthless things as you.
You 'd soon be forc'd (by hunger stung)
To make your dirty meals on dung,
On which such despicable need,
Unpitied, is reduc'd to feed.
Besides, vain selfish Insect, learn,
(If you can right and wrong discern)
That he who, with industrious zeal,
Contributes to the public weal,
By adding to the common good,
His own hath rightly understood.'
  So saying, with a sudden blow,
He laid the noxious vagrant low.
Crush'd in his luxury and pride,
The spunger on the public, died.

THE JACKAL, LEOPARD, AND OTHER BEASTS.

TO A MODERN POLITICIAN.

I GRANT corruption sways mankind;
That interest, too, perverts the mind;
That bribes have blinded common sense,
Foil'd reason, truth, and eloquence:
I grant you, too, our present crimes
Can equal those of former times.
Against plain facts shall I engage,
To vindicate our righteous age?
I know that in a modern fist
Bribes in full energy subsist.
Since then these arguments prevail,
And itching palms are still so frail,
Hence Politicians, you suggest,
Should drive the nail that goes the best;
That it shows parts and penetration,
To ply men with the right temptation.
To this I humbly must dissent,
Premising, no reflection 's meant.
Does justice or the client's sense
Teach lawyers either side's defence?
The fee gives eloquence its spirit;
That only is the client's merit.

Does art, wit, wisdom, or address,
Obtain the prostitute's caress?
The guinea (as in other trades)
From every hand alike persuades.
Man, Scripture says, is prone to evil,
But does that vindicate the devil?
Besides, the more mankind are prone,
The less the devil's parts are shown.
Corruption 's not of modern date;
It hath been tried in every state.
Great knaves of old their pow'r have fenc'd,
By places, pensions, bribes, dispens'd;
By these they gloried in success,
And impudently dar'd oppress;
By these despoticly they sway'd,
And slaves extoll'd the hand that pay'd;
Nor parts nor genius were employ'd,
By these alone were realms destroy'd.
  Now see these wretches in disgrace,
Stript of their treasures, power, and place;
View 'em abandon'd and forlorn,
Expos'd to just reproach and scorn.
What now is all your pride, your boast?
Where are your slaves, your flattering host?
What tongues now feed you with applause?
Where are the champions of your cause?
Now ev'n that very fawning train,
Which shar'd the gleanings of your gain,
Press foremost who shall first accuse
Your selfish jobs, your paltry views,

Your narrow schemes, your breach of trust,
And want of talents to be just.
  What fools were these amidst their pow'r!
How thoughtless of their adverse hour!
What friends were made? A hireling herd,
For temporary votes preferr'd.
Was it these sycophants to get,
Your bounty swell'd a nation's debt?
You 're bit: for these, like Swiss, attend;
No longer pay no longer friend.
  The lion is (beyond dispute)
Allow'd the most majestic brute;
His valour and his generous mind
Prove him superior of his kind:
Yet to jackals (as 'tis averr'd)
Some lions have their power transferr'd;
As if the parts of pimps and spies
To govern forests could suffice.
  Once studious of his private good,
A proud Jackal oppress'd the wood;
To cram his own insatiate jaws,
Invaded property and laws.
The forest groans with discontent,
Fresh wrongs the general hate foment.
The spreading murmurs reach'd his ear;
His secret hours were vex'd with fear.
Night after night he weighs the case;
And feels the terrors of disgrace.
  'By friends (says he) I 'll guard my seat,
By those malicious tongues defeat;

I 'll strengthen power by new allies,
And all my clamorous foes despise.'
 To make the generous beasts his friends,
He cringes, fawns, and condescends;
But those repuls'd his abject court,
And scorn'd oppression to support.
Friends must be had. He can't subsist.
Bribes shall new proselytes enlist;
But these nought weigh'd in honest paws;
For bribes confess a wicked cause:
Yet think not every paw withstands
What hath prevail'd in human hands.
 A tempting turnip's silver skin
Drew a base Hog through thick and thin:
Bought with a Stag's delicious haunch,
The mercenary Wolf was stanch:
The convert Fox grew warm and hearty,
A pullet gain'd him to the party:
The golden pippin in his fist,
A chattering Monkey join'd the list.
 But soon, expos'd to public hate,
The favourite's fall redress'd the state.
The Leopard, vindicating right,
Had brought his secret frauds to light.
As rats, before the mansion falls,
Desert late hospitable walls,
In shoals the servile creatures run,
To bow before the rising sun.
 The Hog with warmth express'd his zeal,
And was for hanging those that steal;

But hop'd, though low, the public hoard
Might half a turnip still afford.
Since saving measures were profest,
A lamb's head was the Wolf's request.
The Fox submitted, if to touch
A gosling would be deem'd too much.
The Monkey thought his grin and chatter
Might ask a nut, or some such matter.
'Ye Hirelings! hence, (the Leopard cries)
Your venal conscience I despise:
He who the public good intends,
By bribes needs never purchase friends.
Who acts this just, this open part,
Is propt by every honest heart.
Corruption now too late has show'd,
That bribes are always ill-bestow'd:
By you your bubbled master's taught,
Time-serving tools, not friends, are bought.'

THE DEGENERATE BEES.

TO THE REV. DR. SWIFT, DEAN OF ST. PATRICK'S.

THOUGH courts the practice disallow,
A friend at all times I'll avow.
In politics I know 'tis wrong;
A friendship may be kept too long:

And what they call the prudent part,
Is to wear interest next the heart.
As the times take a different face,
Old friendships should to new give place.
I know, too, you have many foes,
That owning you is sharing those;
That every knave in every station,
Of high and low denomination,
For what you speak, and what you write,
Dread you at once, and bear you spite.
Such freedoms in your works are shown,
They can't enjoy what's not their own.
All dunces, too, in church and state,
In frothy nonsense show their hate;
With all the petty scribbling crew,
(And those pert sots are not a few)
'Gainst you and Pope their envy spurt:
The booksellers alone are hurt.
Good gods! by what a powerful race
(For blockheads may have pow'r and place)
Are scandals rais'd, and libels writ,
To prove your honesty and wit!
Think with yourself: those worthy men,
You know, have suffer'd by your pen.
From them you've nothing but your due.
From hence, 'tis plain, your friends are few.
Except myself, I know of none,
Besides the wise and good alone.
To set the case in fairer light,
My fable shall the rest recite;

Which (though unlike our present state)
I for the moral's sake relate.
A Bee of cunning, not of parts,
Luxurious, negligent of arts,
Rapacious, arrogant, and vain,
Greedy of power, but more of gain,
Corruption sow'd throughout the hive:
By petty rogues the great ones thrive.
As power and wealth his views supplied;
'Twas seen in overbearing pride.
With him loud impudence had merit;
The Bee of conscience wanted spirit;
And those who follow'd honour's rules
Were laugh'd to scorn for squeamish fools.
Wealth claim'd distinction, favour, grace,
And poverty alone was base.
He treated industry with slight,
Unless he found his profit by 't.
Rights, laws, and liberties, give way.
To bring his selfish schemes in play.
The swarm forgot the common toil,
To share the gleanings of his spoil.
'While vulgar souls, of narrow parts,
Waste life in low mechanic arts;
Let us (says he) to genius born,
The drudgery of our fathers scorn.
The Wasp and Drone, you must agree,
Live with more elegance than we.
Like gentlemen they sport and play;
No business interrupts the day:

Their hours to luxury they give,
And nobly on their neighbours live.'
A stubborn Bee, among the swarm,
With honest indignation warm,
Thus from his cell with zeal replied:
'I slight thy frowns, and hate thy pride.
The laws our native rights protect;
Offending thee, I those respect.
Shall luxury corrupt the hive,
And none against the torrent strive?
Exert the honour of your race;
He builds his rise on your disgrace.
'Tis industry our state maintains,
'Twas honest toil and honest gains
That rais'd our sires to power and fame.
Be virtuous; save yourselves from shame.
Know that in selfish ends pursuing,
You scramble for the public ruin.'
He spoke; and, from his cell dismiss'd,
Was insolently scoff'd and hiss'd:
With him a friend or two resign'd,
Disdaining the degenerate kind.
'These Drones, (says he) these insects vile,
(I treat 'em in their proper style)
May for a time oppress the state:
They own our virtue by their hate;
By that our merits they reveal,
And recommend our public zeal;
Disgrac'd by this corrupted crew,
We're honour'd by the virtuous few.'

THE PACK-HORSE AND THE CARRIER.

TO A YOUNG NOBLEMAN.

BEGIN, my Lord, in early youth,
To suffer, nay, encourage truth ;
And blame me not for disrespect,
If I the flatterer's style reject ;
With that, by menial tongues supplied,
You're daily cocker'd up in pride.
The tree 's distinguish'd by the fruit :
Be virtue then your first pursuit ;
Set your great ancestors in view,
Like them deserve the title too ;
Like them ignoble actions scorn ;
Let virtue prove you greatly born.
Though with less plate their side-board shone,
Their conscience always was their own ;
They ne'er at levees meanly fawn'd,
Nor was their honour yearly pawn'd ;
Their hands, by no corruption stain'd,
The ministerial bribe disdain'd ;
They serv'd the crown with loyal zeal,
Yet, jealous of the publc weal,
They stood the bulwark of our laws,
And wore at heart their country's cause ;

By neither place or pension bought,
They spoke and voted as they thought:
Thus did your sires adorn their seat;
And such alone are truly great.
If you the paths of learning slight,
You 're but a dunce in stronger light.
In foremost rank the coward plac'd,
Is more conspicuously disgrac'd.
If you, to serve a paltry end,
To knavish jobs can condescend,
We pay you the contempt that's due;
In that you have precedence too.
Whence had you this illustrious name?
From virtue and unblemish'd fame.
By birth the name alone descends;
Your honour on yourself depends:
Think not your coronet can hide
Assuming ignorance and pride.
Learning by study must be won;
'Twas ne'er entail'd from son to son.
Superior worth your rank requires;
For that mankind reveres your sires:
If you degenerate from your race,
Their merits heighten your disgrace.
A Carrier, every night and morn,
Would see his horses eat their corn:
This sunk the hostler's vails, 'tis true,
But then his horses had their due.
Were we so cautious in all cases,
Small gain would rise from greater places.

The manger now had all its measure;
He heard the grinding teeth with pleasure;
When all at once confusion rung;
They snorted, jostled, bit, and flung.
A Pack-horse turn'd his head aside,
Foaming, his eye-balls swell'd with pride.
'Good gods! (says he) how hard 's my lot!
Is then my high descent forgot?
Reduc'd to drudgery and disgrace,
(A life unworthy of my race)
Must I, too, bear the vile attacks
Of ragged scrubs and vulgar hacks?
See scurvy Roan, that brute ill-bred,
Dares from the manger thrust my head!
Shall I, who boast a noble line,
On offals of these creatures dine?
Kick'd by old Ball! so mean a foe!
My honour suffers by the blow.
Newmarket speaks my grandsire's fame,
All jockeys still revere his name:
There, yearly, are his triumphs told,
There all his massy plates enroll'd.
Whene'er led forth upon the plain,
You saw him with a livery train;
Returning, too, with laurels crown'd,
You heard the drums and trumpets sound.
Let it then, Sir, be understood,
Respect's my due for I have blood.'
'Vainglorious fool! (the Carrier cried)
Respect was never paid to pride.

Know 'twas thy giddy, wilful heart
Reduc'd thee to this slavish part.
Did not thy headstrong youth disdain
To learn the conduct of the rein?
Thus coxcombs, blind to real merit,
In vicious frolics fancy spirit.
What is 't to me by whom begot?
Thou restive, pert, conceited sot.
Your sires I rev'rence; 'tis their due:
But worthless fool, what's that to you?
Ask all the Carriers on the road,
They'll say thy keeping's ill bestow'd:
Then vaunt no more thy noble race,
That neither mends thy strength or pace.
What profits me thy boast of blood?
An ass hath more intrinsic good.
By outward show let's not be cheated;
An ass should like an ass be treated.'

PAN AND FORTUNE.

TO A YOUNG HEIR.

Soon as your father's death was known,
(As if the estate had been their own)
The gamesters outwardly exprest
The decent joy within your breast:
So lavish in your praise they grew,
As spoke their certain hopes in you.
One counts your income of the year,
How much in ready money clear.
'No house (says he) is more complete;
The garden 's elegant and great.
How fine the park around it lies!
The timber 's of a noble size!
Then, count his jewels and his plate!
Besides, 'tis no entail'd estate.
If cash run low, his lands in fee
Are, or for sale, or mortgage, free.'
Thus they, before you threw the main,
Seem to anticipate their gain.
Would you, when thieves are known abroad,
Bring forth your treasures in the road?
Would not the fool abet the stealth,
Who rashly thus expos'd his wealth?

Yet this you do, whene'er you play
Among the gentlemen of prey.
  Could fools to keep their own contrive,
On what, on whom, could gamesters thrive?
Is it in charity you game,
To save your worthy gang from shame?
Unless you furnish'd daily bread,
Which way could idleness be fed?
Could these professors of deceit
Within the law no longer cheat;
They must run bolder risks for prey,
And strip the traveller on the way.
Thus in your annual rents they share,
And 'scape the noose from year to year.
  Consider, ere you make the bet,
That sum might cross your tailor's debt.
When you the pilfering rattle shake,
Is not your honour, too, at stake?
Must you not by mean lies evade
To-morrow's duns from every trade?
By promises so often paid,
Is yet your tailor's bill defray'd?
Must you not pitifully fawn
To have your butcher's writ withdrawn?
This must be done. In debts of play
Your honour suffers no delay:
And not this year's and next year's rent
The sons of Rapine can content.
  Look round, the wrecks of play behold;
Estates dismember'd, mortgag'd, sold!

Their owners now to jails confin'd,
Show equal poverty of mind.
Some, who the spoil of knaves were made,
Too late attempt to learn their trade.
Some, for the folly of one hour,
Become the dirty tools of pow'r,
And, with the mercenary list,
Upon court-charity subsist.
  You 'll find at last this maxim true,—
Fools are the game which knaves pursue.
  The forest (a whole century's shade)
Must be one wasteful ruin made:
No mercy 's shown to age or kind;
The general massacre is sign'd.
The park, too, shares the dreadful fate,
For duns grow louder at the gate.
Stern clowns, obedient to the 'squire,
(What will not barbarous hands for hire?)
With brawny arms repeat the stroke;
Fall'n are the elm and reverend oak.
Through the long wood loud axes sound,
And Echo groans with every wound.
  To see the desolation spread,
Pan drops a tear, and hangs his head:
His bosom now with fury burns;
Beneath his hoof the dice he spurns.
Cards, too, in peevish passion torn,
The sport of whirling winds are borne.
  'To snails inveterate hate I bear,
Who spoil the verdure of the year;

The caterpillar I detest,
The blooming Spring's voracious pest;
The locust, too, whose ravenous band
Spreads sudden famine o'er the land.
But what are these? The dice's throw
At once hath laid a forest low.
The cards are dealt, the bet is made,
And the wide park hath lost its shade.
Thus is my kingdom's pride defac'd,
And all its ancient glories waste.
All this (he cries) is Fortune's doing:
'Tis thus she meditates my ruin.
By Fortune, that false, fickle jade,
More havoc in one hour is made,
Than all the hungry insect race,
Combin'd, can in an age deface.'
  Fortune, by chance, who near him past,
O'erheard the vile aspersion cast:
  'Why, Pan, (says she) what's all this rant?
'Tis every country-bubble's cant.
Am I the patroness of vice?
Is't I who cog or palm the dice?
Did I the shuffling art reveal,
To mark the cards, or range the deal?
In all the employments men pursue,
I mind the least what gamesters do.
There may (if computation's just)
One now and then my conduct trust.
I blame the fool, for what can I,
When ninety-nine my power defy?

These trust alone their fingers' ends,
And not one stake on me depends.
Whene'er the gaming-board is set,
Two classes of mankind are met;
But if we count the greedy race,
The knaves fill up the greater space.
'Tis a gross error held in schools,
That Fortune always favours fools.
In play it never bears dispute;
That doctrine these fell'd oaks confute.
Then why to me such rancour show?
'Tis Folly, Pan, that is thy foe.
By me his late estate he won,
But he by Folly was undone.'

PLUTUS, CUPID, AND TIME.

Of all the burdens man must bear,
Time seems most galling and severe:
Beneath this grievous load oppress'd,
We daily meet some friend distress'd.
'What can one do? I rose at nine;
'Tis full six hours before we dine:
Six hours! no earthly thing to do!
Would I had doz'd in bed till two.'
A pamphlet is before him spread,
And almost half a page is read;

Tir'd with the study of the day,
The fluttering sheets are toss'd away:
He opes his snuff-box, hums an air,
Then yawns, and stretches in his chair.
'Not twenty, by the minute hand!
Good gods! (says he) my watch must stand?
How muddling 'tis on books to pore!
I thought I'd read an hour or more.
The morning, of all hours, I hate:
One can't contrive to rise too late.'
To make the minutes faster run,
Then, too, his tiresome self to shun,
To the next coffee-house he speeds,
Takes up the news, some scraps he reads.
Sauntering, from chair to chair he trails;
Now drinks his tea, now bites his nails.
He spies a partner of his woe;
By chat afflictions lighter grow;
Each other's grievances they share,
And thus their dreadful hours compare.
Says Tom, 'Since all men must confess,
That time lies heavy, more or less,
Why should it be so hard to get,
Till two, a party at piquet?
Play might relieve the lagging morn:
By cards long wintry nights are borne.
Does not Quadrille amuse the fair,
Night after night, throughout the year?
Vapours and spleen forgot, at play
They cheat uncounted hours away.'

'My case, (says Will) then must be hard,
By want of skill from play debarr'd.
Courtiers kill Time by various ways;
Dependence wears out half their days.
How happy these, whose Time ne'er stands!
Attendance takes it off their hands.
Were it not for this cursed show'r,
The Park had whil'd away an hour.
At court, without or place or view,
I daily lose an hour or two.
It fully answers my design,
When I have pick'd up friends to dine;
The tavern makes our burden light;
Wine puts our time and care to flight.
At six (hard case!) they call to pay.
Where can one go? I hate the play.
From six till ten! unless in sleep,
One cannot spend the hours so cheap.
The comedy 's no sooner done,
But some assembly is begun;
Loitering from room to room I stray,
Converse, but nothing hear or say:
Quite tir'd, from fair to fair I roam.
So soon! I dread the thoughts of home.
From thence, to quicken slow-pac'd Night,
Again my tavern friends invite:
Here, too, our early mornings pass,
Till drowsy sleep retard the glass.'
Thus they their wretched life bemoan,
And make each other's case their own.

Consider, friends, no hour rolls on
But something of your grief is gone.
Were you to schemes of business bred,
Did you the paths of learning tread,
Your hours, your days, would fly too fast;
You 'd then regret the minute past.
Time 's fugitive and light as wind;
'Tis indolence that clogs your mind:
That load from off your spirits shake,
You 'll own, and grieve for your mistake.
A while your thoughtless spleen suspend,
Then read, and (if you can) attend.
As Plutus, to divert his care,
Walk'd forth one morn to take the air,
Cupid o'ertook his strutting pace.
Each star'd upon the stranger's face,
Till recollection set 'em right,
For each knew t' other but by sight.
After some complimental talk,
Time met 'em, bow'd, and join'd their walk:
Their chat on various subjects ran,
But most, what each had done for man.
Plutus assumes a haughty air,
Just like our purse-proud fellows here:
'Let kings, (says he) let cobblers tell,
Whose gifts among mankind excel.
Consider courts; what draws their train?
Think you 'tis loyalty or gain?
That statesman hath the strongest hold,
Whose tool of politics is gold;

By that, in former reigns, 'tis said,
The knave in power hath senates led:
By that alone he sway'd debates,
Enrich'd himself, and beggar'd states.
Forego your boast. You must conclude
That's most esteem'd that's most pursued.
Think, too, in what a woful plight
That wretch must live whose pocket's light.
Are not his hours by want deprest?
Penurious care corrodes his breast:
Without respect, or love, or friends,
His solitary day descends.
'You might, (says Cupid) doubt my parts,
My knowledge, too, in human hearts,
Should I the power of gold dispute,
Which great examples might confute.
I know when nothing else prevails,
Persuasive money seldom fails;
That beauty, too, (like other wares)
Its price, as well as conscience, bears.
Then marriage (as of late profest)
Is but a money-job at best.
Consent, compliance may be sold;
But love's beyond the price of gold.
Smugglers there are who, by retail,
Expose what they call Love to sale;
Such bargains are an arrant cheat:
You purchase flattery and deceit.
Those who true love have ever tried,
(The common cares of life supplied)

No wants endure, no wishes make,
But every real joy partake.
All comfort on themselves depends;
They want nor power, nor wealth, nor friends.
Love, then, hath every bliss in store;
'Tis friendship, and 'tis something more.
Each other every wish they give:
Not to know love is not to live.'
 'Or love, or money, (Time replied)
Were men the question to decide,
Would bear the prize: on both intent,
My boon 's neglected or misspent.
'Tis I who measure vital space,
And deal out years to human race.
Though little priz'd, and seldom sought,
Without me love and gold are nought.
How does the miser time employ?
Did I e'er see him life enjoy?
By me forsook, the hoards he won
Are scatter'd by his lavish son.
By me all useful arts are gain'd;
Wealth, learning, wisdom, is attain'd.
Who then would think (since such my pow'r)
That e'er I knew an idle hour?
So subtle and so swift I fly,
Love 's not more fugitive than I.
Who hath not heard coquettes complain
Of days, months, years, misspent in vain?
For time misus'd they pine and waste,
And love's sweet pleasures never taste.

Those who direct their time aright,
If love or wealth their hopes excite,
In each pursuit fit hours employ'd,
And both by time have been enjoy'd.
How heedless then are mortals grown!
How little is their interest known;
In every view they ought to mind me,
For when once lost they never find me.'
He spoke. The gods no more contest,
And his superior gift confest,
That time (when truly understood)
Is the most precious earthly good.

THE OWL, SWAN, COCK, SPIDER, ASS, AND FARMER.

TO A MOTHER.

Conversing with your sprightly boys,
Your eyes have spoke the Mother's joys.
With what delight I've heard you quote
Their sayings in imperfect note!
  I grant, in body and in mind
Nature appears profusely kind.
Trust not to that. Act you your part;
Imprint just morals on their heart;

Impartially their talents scan:
Just education forms the man.
  Perhaps (their genius yet unknown)
Each lot of life 's already thrown;
That this shall plead, the next shall fight,
The last assert the church's right.
I censure not the fond intent;
But how precarious is th' event!
By talents misapplied and crost,
Consider, all your sons are lost.
  One day (the tale 's by Martial penn'd)
A father thus address'd his friend:
'To train my boy, and call forth sense,
You know I 've stuck at no expense;
I 've tried him in the several arts;
(The lad, no doubt, hath latent parts)
Yet trying all, he nothing knows,
But, crab-like, rather backward goes.
Teach me what yet remains undone;
'Tis your advice shall fix my son.'
  'Sir, (says the friend) I 've weigh'd the matter;
Excuse me, for I scorn to flatter:
Make him (nor think his genius checkt)
A herald or an architect.'
  Perhaps (as commonly 'tis known)
He heard th' advice, and took his own.
  The boy wants wit; he 's sent to school,
Where learning but improves the fool:
The college next must give him parts,
And cram him with the liberal arts.

Whether he blunders at the bar,
Or owes his infamy to war;
Or if by license or degree
The sexton share the doctor's fee;
Or from the pulpit by the hour
He weekly floods of nonsense pour,
We find (th' intent of Nature foil'd)
A tailor or a butcher spoil'd.
  Thus ministers have royal boons
Conferr'd on blockheads and buffoons:
In spite of nature, merit, wit,
Their friends for every post were fit.
  But now let every Muse confess
That merit finds its due success.
The examples of our days regard;
Where 's virtue seen without reward?
Distinguish'd and in place you find
Desert and worth of every kind.
Survey the reverend bench, and see
Religion, learning, piety:
The patron, ere he recommends,
Sees his own image in his friend's.
Is honesty disgrac'd and poor?
What is 't to us what was before?
  We all of times corrupt have heard,
When paltry minions were preferr'd;
When all great offices, by dozens,
Were fill'd by brothers, sons, and cousins.
What matter ignorance and pride?
The man was happily allied.

Provided that his clerk was good,
What though he nothing understood?
In church and state the sorry race
Grew more conspicuous fools in place.
Such heads, as then a treaty made,
Had bungled in the cobbler's trade.
  Consider, patrons, that such elves
Expose your folly with themselves.
'Tis yours, as 'tis the parent's care,
To fix each genius in its sphere.
Your partial hand can wealth dispense,
But never give a blockhead sense.
  An Owl of magisterial air,
Of solemn voice, of brow austere,
Assum'd the pride of human race,
And bore his wisdom in his face;
Not to depreciate learned eyes,
I 've seen a pedant look as wise.
  Within a barn, from noise retir'd,
He scorn'd the world, himself admir'd;
And, like an ancient sage, conceal'd
The follies public life reveal'd.
  Philosophers of old, he read,
Their country's youth to science bred,
Their manners form'd for every station,
And destin'd each his occupation.
When Xenophon, by numbers brav'd,
Retreated, and a people sav'd,
That laurel was not all his own;
The plant by Socrates was sown.

To Aristotle's greater name
The Macedonian ow'd his fame.
 The Athenian bird, with pride replete,
Their talents equall'd in conceit;
And, copying the Socratic rule,
Set up for master of a school.
Dogmatic jargon learnt by heart,
Trite sentences, hard terms of art,
To vulgar ears seem'd so profound,
They fancied learning in the sound.
 The school had fame ; the crowded place
With pupils swarm'd of every race.
With these the Swan's maternal care
Had sent her scarce-fledg'd cygnet heir:
The Hen (though fond and loth to part)
Here lodg'd the darling of her heart:
The Spider, of mechanic kind,
Aspir'd to science more refin'd;
The Ass learnt metaphors and tropes,
But most on music fix'd his hopes.
 The pupils now, advanc'd in age,
Were call'd to tread life's busy stage;
And to the master 'twas submitted,
That each might to his part be fitted:—
 'The Swan (says he) in arms shall shine;
The soldier's glorious toil be thine.'
 'The Cock shall mighty wealth attain:—
Go, seek it on the stormy main.'
 'The court shall be the spider's sphere:
Power, fortune, shall reward him there.'

'In music's art the Ass's fame
Shall emulate Corelli's name.'
Each took the part that he advis'd,
And all were equally despis'd.
A Farmer, at his folly mov'd,
The dull preceptor thus reprov'd:
'Blockhead, (says he) by what you 've done,
One would have thought 'em each your son;
For parents, to their offspring blind,
Consult nor parts nor turn of mind,
But ev'n in infancy decree
What this, what t' other son shall be.
Had you with judgment weigh'd the case,
Their genius thus had fix'd their place;
The Swan had learnt the sailor's art;
The Cock had play'd the soldier's part;
The Spider in the weaver's trade
With credit had a fortune made;
But for the fool, in every class
The blockhead had appear'd an Ass.

THE COOKMAID, TURNSPIT, AND OX.

TO A POOR MAN.

Consider man in every sphere,
Then tell me, is your lot severe?
'Tis murmur, discontent, distrust,
That makes you wretched. God is just.
  I grant that hunger must be fed,
That toil, too, earns thy daily bread.
What then? Thy wants are seen and known,
But every mortal feels his own.
We 're born a restless needy crew:
Show me the happier man than you.
  Adam, though blest above his kind,
For want of social woman pin'd.
Eve's wants the subtle serpent saw,
Her fickle taste transgress'd the law:
Thus fell our sire, and their disgrace
The curse entail'd on human race.
  When Philip's son, by glory led,
Had o'er the globe his empire spread;
When altars to his name were dress'd,
That he was man his tears confess'd.
  The hopes of avarice are check'd:
The proud man always wants respect.

What various wants on power attend?
Ambition never gains its end.
Who hath not heard the rich complain
Of surfeits and corporeal pain?
He, barr'd from every use of wealth,
Envies the ploughman's strength and health.
Another, in a beauteous wife
Finds all the miseries of life:
Domestic jars and jealous fear
Imbitter all his days with care.
This wants an heir; the line is lost:
Why was that vain entail engrost?
Canst thou discern another's mind?
What is 't you envy? Envy 's blind.
Tell Envy, when she would annoy,
That thousands want what you enjoy.
'The dinner must be dish'd at one.
Where 's this vexatious Turnspit gone?
Unless the skulking Cur is caught,
The sirloin 's spoil'd, and I 'm in fault.'
Thus said, (for sure you 'll think it fit
That I the Cookmaid's oaths omit)
With all the fury of a cook,
Her cooler kitchen Nan forsook:
The broomstick o'er her head she waves:
She sweats, she stamps, she puffs, she raves:
The sneaking Cur before her flies;
She whistles, calls; fair speech she tries.
These nought avail. Her choler burns;
The fist and cudgel threat by turns:

With hasty stride she presses near;
He slinks aloof, and howls with fear.
'Was ever Cur so curs'd! (he cried)
What star did at my birth preside!
Am I for life by compact bound
To tread the wheel's eternal round?
Inglorious task! of all our race
No slave is half so mean and base.
Had fate a kinder lot assign'd,
And form'd me of the lap-dog kind,
I then, in higher life employ'd,
Had indolence and ease enjoy'd;
And, like a gentleman, carest,
Had been the lady's favourite guest:
Or were I sprung from spaniel line,
Was his sagacious nostril mine,
By me, their never-erring guide,
From wood and plain their feasts supplied,
Knights, squires, attendant on my pace,
Had shar'd the pleasures of the chase.
Endued with native strength and fire,
Why call'd I not the lion sire?
A lion! such mean views I scorn:
Why was I not of woman born?
Who dares with reason's power contend?
On man we brutal slaves depend:
To him all creatures tribute pay,
And luxury employs his day.'
An Ox by chance o'erheard his moan,
And thus rebuk'd the lazy drone:

'Dare you at partial Fate repine?
How kind's your lot compar'd with mine!
Decreed to toil, the barbarous knife
Hath sever'd me from social life;
Urg'd by the stimulating goad,
I drag the cumbrous wagon's load:
'Tis mine to tame the stubborn plain,
Break the stiff soil, and house the grain;
Yet I without a murmur bear
The various labours of the year.
But then, consider, that one day
(Perhaps the hour's not far away)
You, by the duties of your post,
Shall turn the spit when I'm the roast;
And for reward shall share the feast,
I mean, shall pick my bones at least.'
'Till now (the astonish'd Cur replies)
I look'd on all with envious eyes.
How false we judge by what appears!
All creatures feel their several cares.
If thus yon mighty beast complains,
Perhaps man knows superior pains.
Let envy then no more torment:
Think on the Ox, and learn content.'
Thus said, close following at her heel,
With cheerful heart he mounts the wheel.

THE

RAVENS, SEXTON, AND EARTH-WORM.

TO LAURA.

LAURA, methinks you're over nice.
True ; flattery is a shocking vice ;
Yet sure, whene'er the praise is just,
One may commend without disgust.
Am I a privilege denied,
Indulg'd by every tongue beside ?
How singular are all your ways !
A woman, and averse to praise !
If 'tis offence such truths to tell,
Why do your merits thus excel ?
  Since then I dare not speak my mind,
A truth conspicuous to mankind ;
Though in full lustre every grace
Distinguish your celestial face ;
Though beauties of inferior ray
(Like stars before the orb of day)
Turn pale and fade ; I check my lays,
Admiring what I dare not praise.
  If you the tribute due disdain,
The Muse's mortifying strain

Shall, like a woman in mere spite,
Set beauty in a moral light.
  Though such revenge might shock the ear
Of many a celebrated fair,
I mean that superficial race
Whose thoughts ne'er reach beyond their face,
What's that to you? I but displease
Such ever-girlish ears as these.
Virtue can brook the thoughts of age,
That lasts the same through every stage.
Though you by time must suffer more
Than ever woman lost before,
To age is such indifference shown,
As if your face were not your own.
Were you by Antoninus taught?
Or is it native strength of thought
That thus, without concern or fright,
You view yourself by Reason's light?
  Those eyes, of so divine a ray,
What are they? mouldering, mortal clay.
Those features, cast in heavenly mould,
Shall, like my coarser earth, grow old;
Like common grass the fairest flower
Must feel the hoary season's power.
  How weak, how vain is human pride!
Dares man upon himself confide?
The wretch who glories in his gain,
Amasses heaps on heaps in vain.
Why lose we life in anxious cares,
To lay in hoards for future years?

Can those (when tortur'd by disease)
Cheer our sick heart, or purchase ease?
Can those prolong one gasp of breath,
Or calm the troubled hour of death?
  What's beauty? Call ye that your own?—
A flower that fades as soon as blown.
What's man in all his boast of sway?—
Perhaps the tyrant of a day.
  Alike the laws of life take place
Through every branch of human race:
The monarch of long regal line
Was rais'd from dust as frail as mine.
Can he pour health into his veins?
Or cool the fever's restless pains?
Can he (worn down in Nature's course)
New-brace his feeble nerves with force?
Can he (how vain is mortal power!)
Stretch life beyond the destin'd hour?
  Consider, man; weigh well thy frame;
The king, the beggar is the same.
Dust form'd us all. Each breathes his day,
Then sinks into his native clay.
  Beneath a venerable yew,
That in the lonely churchyard grew,
Two Ravens sate. In solemn croak
Thus one his hungry friend bespoke.
  'Methinks I scent some rich repast;
The savour strengthens with the blast;
Snuff then, the promis'd feast inhale;
I taste the carcass in the gale.

Near yonder trees, the farmer's steed,
From toil and every drudgery freed,
Hath groan'd his last: a dainty treat!
To birds of taste delicious meat.'
  A Sexton, busy at his trade,
To hear their chat suspends his spade.
Death struck him with no farther thought,
Than merely as the fees he brought.
'Was ever two such blundering fowls,
In brains and manners less than owls!
Blockheads, (says he) learn more respect:
Know ye on whom ye thus reflect?
In this same grave (who does me right,
Must own the work is strong and tight)
The 'Squire that yon fair hall possest,
To-night shall lay his bones at rest.
Whence could the gross mistake proceed?
The 'Squire was somewhat fat indeed.
What then? the meanest bird of prey
Such want of sense could ne'er betray;
For sure some difference must be found
(Suppose the smelling organ sound)
In carcasses, (say what we can)
Or where's the dignity of man?'
  With due respect to human race,
The Ravens undertook the case.
In such similitude of scent,
Man ne'er could think reflections meant.
As epicures extol a treat,
And seem their savoury words to eat,

They prais'd dead horse, luxurious food,
The venison of the prescient brood.
  The Sexton's indignation mov'd,
The mean comparison reprov'd;
Their undiscerning palate blam'd,
Which two-legg'd carrion thus defam'd.
  Reproachful speech from either side
The want of argument supplied:
They rail, revile; as often ends
The contest of disputing friends.
  'Hold, (says the fowl) since human pride
With confutation ne'er complied,
Let's state the case, and then refer
The knotty point, for taste may err.'
  As thus he spoke, from out the mould
An Earth-worm, huge of size, unroll'd
His monstrous length: they straight agree
To choose him as their referee:
So to th' experience of his jaws
Each states the merits of the cause.
  He paus'd, and with a solemn tone,
Thus made his sage opinion known:
  'On carcasses of every kind
This maw hath elegantly din'd;
Provoked by luxury or need,
On beast, or fowl, or man, I feed:
Such small distinction's in the savour,
By turns I choose the fancied flavour;
Yet I must own (that human beast)
A glutton is the rankest feast.

Man, cease this boast; for human pride
Hath various tracts to range beside.
The prince who kept the world in awe,
The judge whose dictate fix'd the law;
The rich, the poor, the great, the small,
Are levell'd; death confounds 'em all.
Then think not that we reptiles share
Such cates, such elegance of fare;
The only true and real good
Of man was never vermin's food:
'Tis seated in th' immortal mind;
Virtue distinguishes mankind,
And that (as yet ne'er harbour'd here)
Mounts with the soul we know not where.
So Good-man Sexton, since the case
Appears with such a dubious face,
To neither I the cause determine,
For different tastes please different vermin.'

AY AND NO.

A FABLE.[1]

In Fable all things hold discourse;
Then Words, no doubt, must talk of course.
  Once on a time, near Cannon-row,
Two hostile adverbs, Ay and No,

[1] Taken from the Miscellanies, published by Swift and Pope.

Were hastening to the field of fight,
And front to front stood opposite;
Before each general join'd the van,
Ay, the more courteous knight, began:
 'Stop, peevish Particle! beware!
I'm told you are not such a bear,
But sometimes yield when offer'd fair.
Suffer yon folks a while to tattle;
'Tis we who must decide the battle.
Whene'er we war on yonder stage,
With various fate and equal rage,
The nation trembles at each blow
That No gives Ay, and Ay gives No;
Yet in expensive long contention,
We gain nor office, grant, or pension.
Why then should kinsfolk quarrel thus?
(For two of you make one of us.)
To some wise statesman let us go,
Where each his proper use may know:
He may admit two such commanders,
And make those wait who serv'd in Flanders.
Let's quarter on a great man's tongue,
A treasury lord, not Maister Y———g.
Obsequious at his high command,
Ay shall march forth to tax the land;
Impeachments No can best resist,
And Ay support the Civil list:
Ay, quick as Cæsar, wins the day,
And No, like Fabius, by delay.
Sometimes in mutual sly disguise,

Let Ay's seem No's, and No's seem Ay's;
Ay's be in courts denials meant,
And No's in bishops' give consent.'
  Thus Ay propos'd—and, for reply,
No, for the first time, answer'd 'Ay!'
They parted with a thousand kisses,
And fight e'er since for pay, like Swisses.

RURAL SPORTS.

A GEORGIC.

IN TWO CANTOS.

RURAL SPORTS.

INSCRIBED TO MR. POPE.

—Securi prælia ruris
Pandimus. NEMESIAN.

CANTO I.

YOU, who the sweets of rural life have known,
Despise th' ungrateful hurry of the Town;
In Windsor groves your easy hours employ,
And undisturb'd, yourself and Muse enjoy:
Thames listens to thy strains, and silent flows,
And no rude wind through rustling osiers blows,
While all his wondering nymphs around thee throng,
To hear the Sirens warble in thy song.
But I, who ne'er was bless'd by Fortune's hand,
Nor brighten'd ploughshares in paternal land;
Long in the noisy Town have been immur'd,
Respir'd its smoke, and all its cares endur'd;
Where news and politics divide mankind,
And schemes of state involve th' uneasy mind;
Faction embroils the world, and every tongue
Is mov'd by flattery, or with scandal hung:

Friendship, for sylvan shades, the palace flies,
Where all must yield to interest's dearer ties;
Each rival Machiavel with envy burns,
And honesty forsakes them all by turns;
While calumny upon each party 's thrown,
Which both promote, and both alike disown.
Fatigu'd at last, a calm retreat I chose,
And sooth'd my harass'd mind with sweet repose,
Where fields, and shades, and the refreshing clime,
Inspire the sylvan song, and prompt my rhyme.
My Muse shall rove through flowery meads and plains,
And deck with Rural Sports her native strains,
And the same road ambitiously pursue,
Frequented by the Mantuan swain and you.
'Tis not that Rural Sports alone invite,
But all the grateful country breathes delight;
Here blooming Health exerts her gentle reign,
And strings the sinews of th' industrious swain.
Soon as the morning lark salutes the day,
Through dewy fields I take my frequent way,
Where I behold the farmer's early care,
In the revolving labours of the year.
When the fresh Spring in all her state is crown'd,
And high luxuriant grass o'erspreads the ground,
The labourer with the bending scythe is seen,
Shaving the surface of the waving green;
Of all her native pride disrobes the land,
And meads lays waste before his sweeping hand;

While with the mounting sun the meadow glows,
The fading herbage round he loosely throws;
But if some sign portend a lasting shower,
The experienc'd swain foresees the coming hour,
His sun-burnt hands the scattering fork forsake,
And ruddy damsels ply the saving rake;
In rising hills the fragrant harvest grows,
And spreads along the field in equal rows.
Now when the height of heaven bright Phœbus gains,
And level rays cleave wide the thirsty plains,
When heifers seek the shade and cooling lake,
And in the middle pathway basks the snake,
O lead me, guard me from the sultry hours!
Hide me, ye Forests! in your closest bowers:
Where the tall oak his spreading arms entwines,
And with the beech a mutual shade combines;
Where flows the murmuring brook, inviting dreams,
Where bordering hazel overhangs the streams,
Whose rolling current winding round and round,
With frequent falls makes all the wood resound,
Upon the mossy couch my limbs I cast,
And ev'n at noon the sweets of evening taste.
Here I peruse the Mantuan's Georgic strains,
And learn the labours of Italian swains;
In every page I see new landscapes rise,
And all Hesperia opens to my eyes:
I wander o'er the various rural toil,
And know the nature of each different soil.

This waving field is gilded o'er with corn,
That, spreading trees with blushing fruit adorn;
Here I survey the purple vintage grow,
Climb round the poles, and rise in graceful row:
Now I behold the steed curvet and bound,
And paw with restless hoof the smoking ground:
The dewlap'd bull now chafes along the plain,
While burning love ferments in every vein;
His well-arm'd front against his rival aims,
And by the dint of war his mistress claims:
The careful insect midst his works I view,
Now from the flowers exhaust the fragrant dew:
With golden treasures load his little thighs,
And steer his distant journey through the skies;
Some against hostile drones the hive defend,
Others with sweets the waxen cells distend;
Each in the toil his destin'd office bears,
And in the little bulk a mighty soul appears.
  Or when the ploughman leaves the task of day,
And trudging homeward whistles on the way;
When the big-udder'd cows with patience stand,
Waiting the strokings of the damsel's hand;
No warbling cheers the woods; the feather'd choir
To court kind slumbers to their sprays retire;
When no rude gale disturbs the sleeping trees,
Nor aspen leaves confess the gentlest breeze;
Engag'd in thought, to Neptune's bounds I stray,
To take my farewell of the parting day;
Far in the deep the sun his glory hides,
A streak of gold the sea and sky divides;

The purple clouds their amber linings show,
And edg'd with flame rolls every wave below;
Here pensive I behold the fading light,
And o'er the distant billow lose my sight.
  Now Night in silent state begins to rise,
And twinkling orbs bestrow the uncloudy skies:
Her borrow'd lustre growing Cynthia lends,
And on the main a glittering path extends;
Millions of worlds hang in the spacious air,
Which round their suns their annual circle
    steer;
Sweet contemplation elevates my sense,
While I survey the works of Providence.
O could the Muse in loftier strains rehearse,
The glorious Author of the universe,
Who reins the winds, gives the vast ocean bounds,
And circumscribes the floating worlds their rounds,
My soul should overflow in songs of praise,
And my Creator's name inspire my lays!
  As in successive course the seasons roll,
So circling pleasures recreate the soul.
When genial Spring a living warmth bestows,
And o'er the year her verdant mantle throws,
No swelling inundation hides the grounds,
But crystal currents glide within their bounds;
The finny brood their wonted haunts forsake,
Float in the sun, and skim along the lake;
With frequent leap they range the shallow
    streams,
Their silver coats reflect the dazzling beams:

Now let the fisherman his toils prepare,
And arm himself with every watery snare;
His hooks, his lines, peruse with careful eye,
Increase his tackle, and his rod re-tie.
When floating clouds their spongy fleeces drain,
Troubling the streams with swift-descending rain,
And waters tumbling down the mountain's side,
Bear the loose soil into the swelling tide,
Then, soon as vernal gales begin to rise,
And drive the liquid burden through the skies,
The fisher to the neighbouring current speeds;
Whose rapid surface purls, unknown to weeds;
Upon a rising border of the brook
He sits him down, and ties the treacherous hook;
Now expectation cheers his eager thought,
His bosom glows with treasures yet uncaught;
Before his eyes a banquet seems to stand,
Where every guest applauds his skilful hand.
Far up the stream the twisted hair he throws,
Which down the murmuring current gently flows
When if or chance or hunger's powerful sway
Directs the roving trout this fatal way,
He greedily sucks in the twining bait,
And tugs and nibbles the fallacious meat:
Now, happy fisherman; now twitch the line!
How thy rod bends! behold, the prize is thine!
Cast on the bank, he dies, with gasping pains,
And trickling blood his silver mail distains.
You must not every worm promiscuous use:
Judgment will tell thee proper bait to choose;

The worm that draws a long immoderate size
The trout abhors, and the rank morsel flies;
And if too small, the naked fraud 's in sight,
And fear forbids, while hunger does invite.
Those baits will best reward the fisher's pains,
Whose polish'd tails a shining yellow stains;
Cleanse them from filth, to give a tempting gloss,
Cherish the sullied reptile race with moss;
Amid the verdant bed they twine, they toil,
And from their bodies wipe their native soil.
But when the sun displays his glorious beams,
And shallow rivers flow with silver streams,
Then the deceit the scaly breed survey,
Bask in the sun, and look into the day:
You now a more delusive art must try,
And tempt their hunger with the curious fly.
To frame the little animal, provide
All the gay hues that wait on female pride:
Let Nature guide thee; sometimes golden wire
The shining bellies of the fly require;
The peacock's plumes thy tackle must not fail,
Nor the dear purchase of the sable's tail.
Each gaudy bird some slender tribute brings,
And lends the growing insect proper wings:
Silks of all colours must their aid impart,
And every fur promote the fisher's art.
So the gay lady, with expensive care,
Borrows the pride of land, of sea, and air;

Furs, pearls, and plumes, the glittering thing displays,
Dazzles our eyes, and easy hearts betrays.
Mark well the various seasons of the year,
How the succeeding insect-race appear;
In this revolving moon one colour reigns,
Which in the next the fickle trout disdains.
Oft have I seen a skilful angler try
The various colours of the treacherous fly;
When he with fruitless pain hath skimm'd the brook,
And the coy fish rejects the skipping hook,
He shakes the boughs that on the margin grow,
Which o'er the stream a waving forest throw,
When if an insect fall, (his certain guide)
He gently takes him from the whirling tide,
Examines well his form with curious eyes,
His gaudy vest, his wings, his horns, and size;
Then round his hook the chosen fur he winds,
And on the back a speckled feather binds;
So just the colours shine through every part,
That Nature seems to live again in Art.
Let not thy wary step advance too near,
While all thy hope hangs on a single hair;
The new-form'd insect on the water moves,
The speckled trout the curious snare approves;
Upon the curling surface let it glide,
With natural motion from thy hand supplied,
Against the stream now let it gently play,
Now in the rapid eddy roll away:

The scaly shoals float by, and, seiz'd with fear,
Behold their fellows tost in thinner air;
But soon they leap, and catch the swimming bait,
Plunge on the hook, and share an equal fate.
When a brisk gale against the current blows,
And all the watery plain in wrinkles flows,
Then let the fisherman his art repeat,
Where bubbling eddies favour the deceit.
If an enormous salmon chance to spy,
The wanton errors of the floating fly,
He lifts his silver gills above the flood,
And greedily sucks in the unfaithful food,
Then downward plunges with the fraudful prey,
And bears with joy the little spoil away:
Soon in smart pain he feels the dire mistake,
Lashes the wave, and beats the foamy lake;
With sudden rage he now aloft appears,
And in his eye convulsive anguish bears;
And now again, impatient of the wound,
He rolls and wreathes his shining body round;
Then headlong shoots beneath the dashing tide,
The trembling fins the boiling wave divide:
Now hope exalts the fisher's beating heart,
Now he turns pale, and fears his dubious art;
He views the tumbling fish with longing eyes,
While the line stretches with the unwieldy prize;
Each motion humours with his steady hands,
And one slight hair the mighty bulk commands;
Till tir'd at last, despoil'd of all his strength,
The game athwart the stream unfolds his length.

He now, with pleasure, views the gasping prize
Gnash his sharp teeth, and roll his blood-shot eyes;
Then draws him to the shore, with artful care,
And lifts his nostrils in the sickening air:
Upon the burden'd stream he floating lies,
Stretches his quivering fins, and gasping dies.
  Would you preserve a numerous finny race?
Let your fierce dogs the ravenous otter chase:
The amphibious monster ranges all the shores,
Darts through the waves, and every haunt explores:
Or let the gin his roving steps betray,
And save from hostile jaws the scaly prey.
  I never wander where the bordering reeds
O'erlook the muddy stream, whose tangling weeds
Perplex the fisher; I nor choose to bear
The thievish nightly net nor barbed spear;
Nor drain I ponds, the golden carp to take,
Nor trowl for pikes, dispeoplers of the lake.
Around the steel no tortur'd worm shall twine,
No blood of living insect stain my line:
Let me, less cruel, cast the feather'd hook
With pliant rod athwart the pebbled brook,
Silent along the mazy margin stray,
And with the fur-wrought fly delude the prey.

CANTO II.

Now, sporting Muse! draw in the flowing reins,
Leave the clear streams awhile for sunny plains.
Should you the various arms and toils rehearse,
And all the fisherman adorn thy verse!
Should you the wide-encircling net display,
And in its spacious arch enclose the sea,
Then haul the plunging load upon the land,
And with the sole and turbot hide the sand;
It would extend the growing theme too long,
And tire the reader with the watery song.
  Let the keen hunter from the chase refrain,
Nor render all the ploughman's labour vain,
When Ceres pours out plenty from her horn,
And clothes the fields with golden ears of corn.
Now, now, ye Reapers! to your task repair;
Haste, save the product of the bounteous year:
To the wide-gathering hook long furrows yield,
And rising sheaves extend through all the field.
  Yet if for slyvan sports thy bosom glow,
Let thy fleet greyhound urge his flying foe.
With what delight the rapid course I view!
How does my eye the circling race pursue!
He snaps deceitful air with empty jaws,
The subtle hare darts swift beneath his paws:
She flies, he stretches: now with nimble bound
Eager he presses on, but overshoots his ground:

She turns, he winds, and soon regains the way,
Then tears with gory mouth the screaming prey.
What various sport does rural life afford!
What unbought dainties heap the wholesome board!

Nor less the spaniel, skilful to betray,
Rewards the fowler with the feather'd prey.
Soon as the labouring horse, with swelling veins,
Hath safely hous'd the farmer's doubtful gains,
To sweet repast the unwary partridge flies,
With joy amid the scatter'd harvest lies;
Wandering in plenty, danger he forgets,
Nor dreads the slavery of entangling nets,
The subtle dog scours with sagacious nose
Along the field, and snuffs each breeze that blows;
Against the wind he takes his prudent way,
While the strong gale directs him to the prey:
Now the warm scent assures the covey near,
He treads with caution, and he points with fear;
Then (lest some sentry fowl the fraud descry,
And bids his fellows from the danger fly)
Close to the ground in expectation lies,
Till in the snare the fluttering covey rise.
Soon as the blushing light begins to spread,
And glancing Phœbus gilds the mountain's head,
His early flight the ill-fated partridge takes,
And quits the friendly shelter of the brakes:
Or when the sun casts a declining ray,
And drives his chariot down the western way,

Let your obsequious ranger search around,
Where yellow stubble withers on the ground;
Nor will the roving spy direct in vain,
But numerous coveys gratify thy pain.
When the meridian sun contracts the shade,
And frisking heifers seek the cooling glade;
Or when the country floats with sudden rains,
Or driving mists deface the moisten'd plains,
In vain his toils the unskilful fowler tries,
While in thick woods the feeding partridge lies.
Nor must the sporting verse the gun forbear,
But what's the fowler's be the Muse's care.
See how the well-taught pointer leads the way:
The scent grows warm; he stops; he springs the prey:
The fluttering coveys from the stubble rise,
And on swift wing divide the sounding skies;
The scattering lead pursues the certain sight,
And death in thunder overtakes their flight.
Cool breathes the morning air, and Winter's hand
Spreads wide her hoary mantle o'er the land;
Now to the copse thy lesser spaniel take,
Teach him to range the ditch and force the brake;
Not closest coverts can protect the game:
Hark! the dog opens; take thy certain aim:
The woodcock flutters; how he wavering flies!
The wood resounds: he wheels, he drops, he dies.
The towering hawk let future poets sing,
Who terror bears upon his soaring wing;

Let them on high the frighted hern survey,
And lofty numbers paint their airy fray.
Nor shall the mounting lark the Muse detain,
That greets the morning with his early strain;
When, midst his song, the twinkling glass betrays;
While from each angle flash the glancing rays,
And in the sun the transient colours blaze,
Pride lures the little warbler from the skies:
The light-enamour'd bird deluded dies.
But still the chase, a pleasing task, remains;
The hound must open in these rural strains.
Soon as Aurora drives away the night,
And edges eastern clouds with rosy light,
The healthy huntsman, with the cheerful horn,
Summons the dogs, and greets the dappled Morn:
The jocund thunder wakes the enliven'd hounds,
They rouse from sleep, and answer sounds for sounds:
Wide through the furzy field their route they take,
Their bleeding bosoms force the thorny brake:
The flying game their smoking nostrils trace,
No bounding hedge obstructs their eager pace;
The distant mountains echo from afar,
And hanging woods resound the flying war:
The tuneful noise the sprightly courser hears,
Paws the green turf, and pricks his trembling ears:
The slacken'd rein now gives him all his speed,
Back flies the rapid ground beneath the steed;

Hills, dales, and forests, far behind remain,
While the warm scent draws on the deep-mouth'd train.
Where shall the trembling hare a shelter find?
Hark! death advances in each gust of wind!
New stratagems and doubling wiles she tries,
Now circling turns, and now at large she flies;
Till, spent at last, she pants, and heaves for breath,
Then lays her down, and waits devouring death.
But stay, adventurous Muse! .hast thou the force
To wind the twisted horn, to guide the horse?
To keep thy seat unmov'd hast thou the skill,
O'er the high gate and down the headlong hill?
Canst thou the stag's laborious chase direct,
Or the strong fox through all his arts detect?
The theme demands a more experienc'd lay;
Ye mighty Hunters! spare this weak essay.
O happy plains! remote from war's alarms,
And all the ravages of hostile arms!
And happy shepherds! who, secure from fear,
On open downs preserve your fleecy care!
Whose spacious barns groan with increasing store,
And whirling flails disjoint the cracking floor:
No barbarous soldier, bent on cruel spoil,
Spreads desolation o'er your fertile soil;
No trampling steed lays waste the ripen'd grain,
Nor crackling fires devour the promis'd gain;

No flaming beacons cast their blaze afar,
The dreadful signal of invasive war;
No trumpet's clangor wounds the mother's ear,
And calls the lover from his swooning fair.
What happiness the rural maid attends,
In cheerful labour while each day she spends!
She gratefully receives what Heav'n has sent,
And, rich in poverty, enjoys content:
(Such happiness, and such unblemish'd fame,
Ne'er glad the bosom of the courtly dame)
She never feels the spleen's imagin'd pains,
Nor melancholy stagnates in her veins;
She never loses life in thoughtless ease,
Nor on the velvet couch invites disease;
Her home-spun dress in simple neatness lies,
And for no glaring equipage she sighs:
Her reputation, which is all her boast,
In a malicious visit ne'er was lost:
No midnight masquerade her beauty wears,
And health, not paint, the fading bloom repairs.
If love's soft passion in her bosom reign,
An equal passion warms her happy swain.
No homebred jars her quiet state control,
Not watchful jealousy torments her soul:
With secret joy she sees her little race
Hang on her breast, and her small cottage grace;
The fleecy ball their little fingers cull,
Or from the spindle draw the lengthening wool.
Thus flow her hours with constant peace of mind,
Till age the latest thread of life unwind.

Ye happy Fields! unknown to noise and strife,
The kind rewarders of industrious life;
Ye shady Woods! where once I us'd to rove,
Alike indulgent to the Muse and love;
Ye murmuring Streams! that in meanders roll,
The sweet composers of the pensive soul,
Farewell.—The City calls me from your bow'rs:
Farewell, amusing thoughts and peaceful hours!

TRIVIA:

OR, THE ART OF

WALKING THE STREETS OF LONDON.

IN THREE BOOKS.

Quo te, Mœri, pedes? An, quo via ducit, in urbem?

VIRG.

ADVERTISEMENT.

THE world, I believe, will take so little notice of me, that I need not take much of it. The critics may see, by this Poem, that I walk on foot, which probably may save me from their envy. I should be sorry to raise that passion in men whom I am so much obliged to, since they allow me an honour hitherto only shown to better writers,—that of denying me to be the author of my own works.

Gentlemen, if there be any thing in this Poem good enough to displease you, and if it be any advantage to you to ascribe it to some person of greater merit; I shall acquaint you, for your comfort, that, among many other obligations, I owe several hints of it to Dr. Swift; and if you will so far continue your favour as to write against it, I beg you to oblige me in accepting the following motto:

—— Non tu, in Triviis, indocte, solebas
Stridenti miserum stipula disperdere carmen?

TRIVIA.

BOOK I.

OF THE IMPLEMENTS FOR WALKING THE STREETS, AND SIGNS OF THE WEATHER.

THROUGH winter streets to steer your course
aright,
How to walk clean by day, and safe by night,
How jostling crowds, with prudence to decline,
When to assert the wall, and when resign,
I sing: thou, Trivia! goddess, aid my song,
Through spacious streets conduct thy bard along;
By thee transported, I securely stray
Where winding alleys lead the doubtful way,
The silent court and opening square explore,
And long perplexing lanes untrod before.
To pave thy realm, and smooth the broken ways,
Earth from her womb a flinty tribute pays;
For thee the sturdy paver thumps the ground,
Whilst every stroke his labouring lungs resound;
For thee the scavenger bids kennels glide
Within their bounds, and heaps of dirt subside.
My youthful bosom burns with thirst of fame,
From the great theme to build a glorious name,

To tread in paths to ancient bards unknown,
And bind my temples with a civic crown;
But more, my country's love demands the lays;
My country's be the profit; mine the praise.
  When the black youth at chosen stands rejoice,
And 'Clean your shoes,' resounds from every voice;
When late their miry sides stage-coaches show,
And their stiff horses through the Town move slow;
When all the Mall in leafy ruin lies,
And damsels first renew their oyster cries,
Then let the prudent walker shoes provide,
Not of the Spanish or Morocco hide;
The wooden heel may raise the dancer's bound,
And with the scallop'd top his step be crown'd:
Let firm, well-hammer'd soles protect thy feet
Through freezing snows, and rains, and soaking sleet.
Should the big last extend the shoe too wide,
Each stone will wrench the unwary step aside;
The sudden turn may stretch the swelling vein,
Thy cracking joint unhinge, or ankle sprain;
And when too short the modish shoes are worn,
You'll judge the seasons by your shooting corn.
  Nor should it prove thy less important care
To choose a proper coat for winter's wear.
Now in thy trunk thy D'Oily habit fold,
The silken drugget ill can fence the cold;

The freeze's spongy nap is soak'd with rain,
And showers soon drench the camlet's cockled grain;
True Whitney[1] broad-cloth, with its shag unshorn,
Unpierc'd is in the lasting tempest worn:
Be this the horseman's fence; for who would wear
Amid the Town the spoils of Russia's bear?
Within the roquelaure's clasp thy hands are pent,
Hands that stretch'd forth invading harms prevent.
Let the loop'd Bavaroy the fop embrace,
Or his deep cloak bespatter'd o'er with lace:
That garment best the winter's rage defends,
Whose shapeless form in ample plaits depends;
By various names[2] in various counties known,
Yet held in all the true Surtout alone;
Be thine of kersey firm, though small the cost,
Then brave unwet the rain, unchill'd the frost.
If the strong cane support thy walking hand,
Chairmen no longer shall the wall command:
Ev'n sturdy carmen shall thy nod obey,
And rattling coaches stop to make thee way:
This shall direct thy cautious tread aright,
Though not one glaring lamp enliven night.
Let beaux their canes, with amber tipt produce;
Be theirs for empty show, but thine for use.
In gilded chariots while they loll at ease,
And lazily insure a life's disease;

1 A town in Oxfordshire. 2 A Joseph, a Wraprascal &c.

While softer chairs the tawdry load convey
To court, to White's,[8] assemblies, or the play;
Rosy-complexion'd Health thy steps attends,
And exercise thy lasting youth defends.
Imprudent men Heaven's choicest gifts profane.
Thus some beneath their arm support the cane;
The dirty point oft checks the careless pace,
And miry spots thy clean cravat disgrace;
O! may I never such misfortune meet,
May no such vicious walkers crowd the street;
May Providence o'ershade me with her wings,
While the bold Muse experienc'd dangers sings.
Not that I wander from my native home,
And (tempting perils) foreign cities roam.
Let Paris be the theme of Gallia's Muse,
Where slavery treads the street in wooden shoes:
Nor do I rove in Belgia's frozen clime,
And teach the clumsy boor to skate in rhyme,
Where, if the warmer clouds in rain descend,
No miry ways industrious steps offend,
The rushing flood from sloping pavements pours,
And blackens the canals with dirty showers.
Let others Naples' smoother streets rehearse,
And with proud Roman structures grace their verse,
Where frequent murders wake the night with groans,
And blood in purple torrents dyes the stones:

[8] White's chocolate house, in St. James's Street.

Nor shall the Muse through narrow Venice stray,
Where gondolas their painted oars display.
O happy streets! to rumbling wheels unknown,
No carts, no coaches, shake the floating town!
Thus was of old Britannia's city bless'd,
Ere pride and luxury her sons possess'd;
Coaches and chariots yet unfashion'd lay,
Nor late invented chairs perplex'd the way:
Then the proud lady tripp'd along the Town,
And tuck'd-up petticoats secur'd her gown,
Her rosy cheek with distant visits glow'd,
And exercise unartful charms bestow'd;
But since in braided gold her foot is bound,
And a long trailing mantua sweeps the ground,
Her shoe disdains the street: the lazy fair
With narrow step affects a limping air.
Now gaudy pride corrupts the lavish age,
And the streets flame with glaring equipage:
The tricking gamester insolently rides,
With Loves and Graces on his chariot sides:
In saucy state the griping broker sits,
And laughs at honesty and trudging wits.
For you, O honest men! these useful lays
The Muse prepares; I seek no other praise.
When sleep is first disturb'd by morning cries,
From sure prognostics learn to know the skies,
Lest you of rheums and coughs at night complain,
Surpris'd in dreary fogs or driving rain.
When suffocating mists obscure the morn,
Let thy worst wig, long us'd to storms, be worn;

This knows the powder'd footman, and with care,
Beneath his flapping hat secures his hair.
Be thou, for every season, justly drest,
Nor brave the piercing frost with open breast;
And when the bursting clouds a deluge pour,
Let thy surtout defend the drenching shower.
  The changing weather certain signs reveal.
Ere winter sheds her snow, or frosts congeal,
You 'll see the coals in brighter flames aspire,
And sulphur tinge with blue the rising fire;
Your tender shins the scorching heat decline,
And at the dearth of coals the poor repine;
Before her kitchen hearth the nodding dame,
In flannel mantle wrapt, enjoys the flame;
Hovering upon her feeble knees she bends,
And all around the grateful warmth ascends.
  Nor do less certain signs the Town advise
Of milder weather and serener skies.
The ladies, gaily dress'd, the Mall adorn
With various dyes, and paint the sunny morn;
The wanton fawns with frisking pleasure range,
And chirping sparrows greet the welcome change:
Not that their minds with greater skill are fraught,[4]
Endued by instinct, or by reason taught;
The seasons operate on every breast:
'Tis hence that fawns are brisk, and ladies drest,

[4] Haud equidem credo, quia sit divinitus illis
Ingenium, aut rerum fato prudentia major.
Virg. Georg. I. 415.

When on his box the nodding coachman snores,
And dreams of fancied fares; when tavern-doors
The chairmen idly crowd, then ne'er refuse
To trust thy busy steps in thinner shoes.
But when the swinging signs your ears offend
With creaking noise, then rainy floods impend;
Soon shall the kennels swell with rapid streams,
And rush in muddy torrents to the Thames.
The bookseller, whose shop 's an open square,
Foresees the tempest, and with early care
Of learning strips the rails: the rowing crew,
To tempt a fare, clothe all their tilts in blue.
On hosiers' poles depending stockings tied,
Flag with the slacken'd gale from side to side.
Church-monuments foretell the changing air;
Then Niobe dissolves into a tear,
And sweats with secret grief. You'll hear the sounds
Of whistling winds ere kennels break their bounds;
Ungrateful odours common-sewers diffuse,
And dropping vaults distil unwholesome dews,
Ere the tiles rattle with the smoking shower,
And spouts on heedless men their torrents pour.
All superstition from thy breast repel:
Let credulous boys, and prattling nurses tell
How, if the festival of Paul be clear,
Plenty from liberal horn shall strow the year;
When the dark skies dissolve in snow or rain,
The labouring hind shall yoke the steer in vain;
But if the threatening winds in tempests roar,
Then War shall bathe her wasteful sword in gore:

How, if on Swithin's feast the welkin lowers,
And every penthouse streams with hasty showers,
Twice twenty days shall clouds their fleeces drain,
And wash the pavements with incessant rain.
Let not such vulgar tales debase thy mind;
Nor Paul nor Swithin rule the clouds and wind.
  If you the precepts of the Muse despise,
And slight the faithful warning of the skies,
Others you 'll see, when all the Town 's afloat,
Wrapt in the embraces of a kersey coat,
Or double-button'd freeze; their guarded feet
Defy the muddy dangers of the street,
While you, with hat unloop'd, the fury dread
Of spouts high streaming, and with cautious tread
Shun every dashing pool; or idly stop,
To seek the kind protection of a shop.
But business summons; now with hasty scud
You jostle for the wall; the spatter'd mud
Hides all thy hose behind; in vain you scour;
Thy wig, alas! uncurl'd, admits the shower:
So fierce Alecto's snaky tresses fell,
When Orpheus charm'd the rigorous powers of hell;
Or thus hung Glaucus' beard, with briny dew
Clotted and strait, when first his amorous view
Surpris'd the bathing fair; the frighted maid
Now stands a rock, transform'd by Circe's aid.
  Good housewives all the winter's rage despise,
Defended by the riding-hood's disguise;
Or, underneath the umbrella's oily shade,
Safe through the wet on clinking pattens tread.

Let Persian dames the umbrella's ribs display,
To guard their beauties from the sunny ray;
Or sweating slaves support the shady load,
When eastern monarchs show their state abroad;
Britain in winter only knows its aid,
To guard from chilly showers the walking maid.
But, O! forget not, Muse! the patten's praise,
That female implement shall grace thy lays;
Say from what art divine the invention came,
And from its origin deduce the name.

Where Lincoln wide extends her fenny soil,
A goodly yeoman liv'd grown white with toil;
One only daughter blest his nuptial bed,
Who from her infant hand the poultry fed:
Martha (her careful mother's name) she bore,
But now her careful mother was no more.
Whilst on her father's knee the damsel play'd,
Patty he fondly call'd the smiling maid;
As years increas'd, her ruddy beauty grew,
And Patty's fame o'er all the village flew.

Soon as the gray-ey'd Morning streaks the skies,
And in the doubtful day the woodcock flies,
Her cleanly pail the pretty housewife bears,
And singing to the distant field repairs;
And when the plains with evening dews are spread,
The milky burden smokes upon her head:
Deep through a miry lane she pick'd her way,
Above her ankle rose the chalky clay.

Vulcan by chance the gloomy maiden spies,
With innocence and beauty in her eyes:

He saw, he lov'd; for yet he ne'er had known
Sweet innocence and beauty meet in one.
Ah! Mulciber! recall thy nuptial vows,
Think on the graces of thy Paphian spouse;
Think how her eyes dart inexhausted charms,
And canst thou leave her bed for Patty's arms?
  The Lemnian Power forsakes the realms above,
His bosom glowing with terrestrial love.
Far in the lane a lonely hut he found,
No tenant ventur'd on the unwholesome ground.
Here smokes his forge, he bares his sinewy arm,
And early strokes the sounding anvil warm:
Around his shop the steely sparkles flew,
As for the steed he shap'd the bending shoe.
  When blue-ey'd Patty near his window came,
His anvil rests, his forge forgets to flame:
To hear his soothing tales she feigns delays;
What woman can resist the force of praise?
  At first she coyly every kiss withstood,
And all her cheek was flush'd with modest blood;
With headless nails he now surrounds her shoes,
To save her steps from rains and piercing dews.
She lik'd his soothing tales, his presents wore,
And granted kisses, but would grant no more.
Yet winter chill'd her feet, with cold she pines,
And on her cheek the fading rose declines;
No more her humid eyes their lustre boast,
And in hoarse sounds her melting voice is lost.
  This Vulcan saw, and in his heavenly thought
A new machine mechanic fancy wrought,

Above the mire her shelter'd steps to raise,
And bear her safely through the wintry ways.
Straight the new engine on his anvil glows,
And the pale virgin on the patten rose.
No more her lungs are shook with dropping rheums,
And on her cheek reviving beauty blooms.
The god obtain'd his suit: though flattery fail,
Presents with female virtue must prevail.
The patten now supports each frugal dame,
Which from the blue-ey'd Patty takes the name.

BOOK II.

ON WALKING THE STREETS BY DAY.

THUS far the Muse has trac'd, in useful lays,
The proper implements for wintry ways;
Has taught the walker with judicious eyes
To read the various warnings of the skies:
Now venture, Muse! from home to range the Town,
And for the public safety risk thy own.
  For ease and for despatch the morning's best;
No tides of passengers the street molest:
You'll see a draggled damsel here and there,
From Billingsgate her fishy traffic bear:
On doors the sallow milkmaid chalks her gains;
Ah! how unlike the milkmaid of the plains!
Before proud gates attending asses bray,
Or arrogate with solemn pace the way;
These grave physicians, with their milky cheer,
The love-sick maid and dwindling beau repair.
Here rows of drummers stand in martial file,
And with their vellum thunder shake the pile,
To greet the new-made bride: are sounds like these
The proper prelude to a state of peace?

Now Industry awakes her busy sons ;
Full charg'd with news the breathless hawker runs :
Shops open, coaches roll, carts shake the ground,
And all the streets with passing cries resound.
  If cloth'd in black you tread the busy Town,
Or if distinguish'd by the reverend gown,
Three trades avoid. Oft in the mingling press
The barber's apron soils the sable dress :
Shun the perfumer's touch with cautious eye ;
Nor let the baker's step advance too nigh.
Ye walkers, too, that youthful colours wear,
Three sullying trades avoid with equal care.
The little chimney-sweeper skulks along,
And marks with sooty stains the heedless throng :
When small-coal murmurs in the hoarser throat,
From smutty dangers guard thy threaten'd coat ;
The dust-man's cart offends thy clothes and eyes,
When through the street a cloud of ashes flies :
But whether black or lighter dyes are worn,
The chandler's basket, on his shoulder borne,
With tallow spots thy coat : resign the way,
To shun the surly butcher's greasy tray ; [stain,
Butchers ! whose hands are dy'd with blood's foul
And always foremost in the hangman's train.
  Let due civilities be strictly paid ;
The wall surrender to the hooded maid ;
Nor let thy sturdy elbow's hasty rage
Jostle the feeble steps of trembling age :
And when the porter bends beneath his load,
And pants for breath, clear thou the crowded road :

But, above all, the groping blind direct,
And from the pressing throng the lame protect.
You 'll sometimes meet a fop, of nicest tread,
Whose mantling peruke veils his empty head:
At every step he dreads the wall to lose,
And risks, to save a coach, his red-heel'd shoes;
Him, like the miller, pass with caution by,
Lest from his shoulder clouds of powder fly:
But when the bully, with assuming pace,
Cocks his broad hat, edg'd round with tarnish'd lace,
Yield not the way; defy his strutting pride,
And thrust him to the muddy kennel's side:
He never turns again, nor dares oppose,
But mutters coward curses as he goes.
If drawn by business to a street unknown,
Let the sworn porter point thee through the Town.
Be sure observe the signs, for signs remain
Like faithful landmarks to the walking train.
Seek not from 'prentices to learn the way;
Those fabling boys will turn thy steps astray:
Ask the grave tradesman to direct thee right;
He ne'er deceives but when he profits by 't.
Where fam'd St. Giles's ancient limits spread,
An inrail'd column rears its lofty head;
Here to sev'n streets sev'n dials count the day,
And from each other catch the circling ray:
Here oft the peasant, with inquiring face,
Bewilder'd, trudges on from place to place;
He dwells on every sign with stupid gaze,
Enters the narrow alley's doubtful maze;

Tries every winding court and street in vain,
And doubles o'er his weary steps again.
Thus hardy Theseus, with intrepid feet,
Travers'd the dangerous labyrinth of Crete;
But still the wandering passes forc'd his stay,
Till Ariadne's clue unwinds the way:
But do not thou, like that bold chief, confide
Thy venturous footsteps to a female guide;
She 'll lead thee with delusive smiles along,
Dive in thy fob, and drop thee in the throng.
When waggish boys the stunted besom ply,
To rid the slabby pavement, pass not by
Ere thou hast held their hands; some heedless flirt
Will overspread thy calves with spattering dirt.
Where porters hogsheads roll from carts aslope,
Or brewers down steep cellars stretch the rope,
Where counted billets are by carmen tost,
Stay thy rash step, and walk without the post.
What though the gathering mire thy feet be-
smear?
The voice of industry is always near.
Hark! the boy calls thee to his destin'd stand,
And the shoe shines beneath his oily hand.
Here let the Muse, fatigu'd amid the throng,
Adorn her precepts with digressive song;
Of shirtless youths the secret rise to trace,
And show the parent of the sable race.
Like mortal man, great Jove (grown fond of
[change)
Of old was wont this nether world to range

To seek amours; the vice the monarch lov'd
Soon through the wide ethereal court improv'd,
And ev'n the proudest goddess, now and then,
Would lodge a night among the sons of men;
To vulgar deities descends the fashion,
Each, like her betters, had her earthly passion.
Then Cloacina[1] (goddess of the tide
Whose sable streams beneath the city glide)
Indulg'd the modish flame; the Town she rov'd;
A mortal scavenger she saw; she lov'd;
The muddy spots that dried upon his face,
Like female patches, heighten'd every grace:
She gaz'd; she sigh'd: for Love can beauties spy
In what seems faults to every common eye.
  Now had the watchman walk'd his second round,
When Cloacina hears the rumbling sound
Of her brown lover's cart, for well she knows
That pleasing thunder: swift the goddess rose,
And through the streets pursued the distant noise,
Her bosom panting with expected joys,
With the night-wandering harlot's airs she past,
Brush'd near his side, and wanton glances cast:
In the black form of cinder-wench she came,
When love, the hour, the place, had banish'd shame;

[1] Cloacina was a goddess whose image Tatius (a king of the Sabines) found in the common sewer, and not knowing what goddess it was, he called it Cloacina, from the place in which it was found, and paid to it divine honours. *Lactant,* 1, 20. *Minuc. Fel. Oct.* p. 232.

To the dark alley arm in arm they move;
O may no link-boy interrupt their love!
When the pale moon had nine times fill'd her space,
The pregnant goddess (cautious of disgrace)
Descends to earth, but sought no midwife's aid,
Nor midst her anguish to Lucina pray'd;
No cheerful gossip wish'd the mother joy;
Alone, beneath a bulk, she dropt the boy.
The child through various risks in years improved;
At first a beggar's brat, compassion mov'd;
His infant tongue soon learnt the canting art,
Knew all the prayers and whines to touch the heart.
O happy unown'd youths! your limbs can bear
The scorching dog-star and the winter's air,
While the rich infant, nurs'd with care and pain,
Thirsts with each heat and coughs with every rain!
The goddess long had mark'd the child's distress,
And long had sought his sufferings to redress;
She prays the gods to take the fondling's part,
To teach his hands some beneficial art
Practis'd in streets: the gods her suit allow'd,
And made him useful to the walking crowd,
To cleanse the miry feet, and o'er the shoe
With nimble skill the glossy black renew.
Each power contributes to relieve the poor:
With the strong bristles of the mighty boar
Diana forms his brush; the god of day
A tripod gives, amid the crowded way

To raise the dirty foot, and ease his toil;
Kind Neptune fills his vase with fetid oil
Prest from the enormous whale: the god of fire,
From whose dominions smoky clouds aspire,
Among these generous presents joins his part,
And aids with soot the new japanning art.
Pleas'd she receives the gifts; she downward glides,
Lights in Fleet-ditch, and shoots beneath the tides.

Now dawns the morn, the sturdy lad awakes,
Leaps from his stall, his tangled hair he shakes,
Then leaning o'er the rails, he musing stood,
And view'd below the black canal of mud,
Where common sewers a lulling murmur keep,
Whose torrents rush from Holborn's fatal steep;
Pensive through idleness, tears flow'd apace,
Which eas'd his loaded heart, and wash'd his face;
At length he sighing cried, 'That boy is blest,
Whose infant lips have drain'd a mother's breast;
But happier far are those, (if such be known)
Whom both a father and a mother own;
But I, alas! hard Fortune's utmost scorn,
Who ne'er knew parent, was an orphan born!
Some boys are rich by birth beyond all wants,
Belov'd by uncles, and kind good old aunts; [bear,
When time comes round, a Christmas-box they
And one day makes them rich for all the year.
Had I the precepts of a father learn'd,
Perhaps I then the coachman's fare had earn'd;
For lesser boys can drive: I thirsty stand,
And see the double flagon charge their hand;

See them puff off the froth, and gulp a main,
While with dry tongue I lick my lips in vain.'
  While thus he fervent prays, the heaving tide
In widen'd circles beats on either side;
The goddess rose amid the inmost round,
With wither'd turnip-tops her temples crown'd;
Low reach'd her dripping tresses, lank, and black
As the smooth jet, or glossy ravens' back;
Around her waist a circling eel was twin'd,
Which bound her robe, that hung in rags behind:
Now beckoning to the boy, she thus begun;
'Thy prayers are granted; weep no more, my son;
Go thrive. At some frequented corner stand;
This brush I give thee, grasp it in thy hand;
Temper the soot within this vase of oil,
And let the little tripod aid thy toil;
On this methinks I see the walking crew,
At thy request, support the miry shoe;
The foot grows black that was with dirt imbrown'd,
And in thy pocket jingling halfpence sound.'
The goddess plunges swift beneath the flood,
And dashes all around her showers of mud:
The youth straight chose his post; the labour plied,
Where branching streets from Charing-cross divide;
His treble voice resounds along the Mews,
And Whitehall echoes — 'Clean your honour's shoes.'
  Like the sweet ballad, this amusing lay
Too long detains the walker on his way;

While he attends, new dangers round him throng;
The busy City asks instructive song.

Where elevated o'er the gaping crowd,
Clasp'd in the board the perjur'd head is bow'd,
Betimes retreat; here, thick as hailstones pour,
Turnips and half-hatch'd eggs (a mingled shower)
Among the rabble rain; some random throw
May with the trickling yolk thy cheek o'erflow.

Though expedition bids, yet never stray
Where no rang'd posts defend the rugged way:
Here laden carts with thundering wagons meet,
Wheels clash with wheels, and bar the narrow street;
The lashing whip resounds, the horses strain,
And blood in anguish bursts the swelling vein.
O barbarous Men! your cruel breasts assuage;
Why vent ye on the generous steed your rage?
Does not his service earn your daily bread?
Your wives, your children, by his labours fed!
If, as the Samian taught, the soul revives,
And, shifting seats, in other bodies lives,
Severe shall be the brutal coachman's change,
Doom'd in a hackney horse the Town to range;
Carmen, transform'd, the groaning load shall draw,
Whom other tyrants with the lash shall awe.

Who would of Watling-street the dangers share,
When the broad pavement of Cheapside is near?
Or who that rugged street would traverse o'er,
That stretches, O Fleet-ditch! from thy black shore

To the Tower's moated walls?[2] here steams ascend
That, in mix'd fumes, the wrinkled nose offend.
Where chandlers' caldrons boil; where fishy prey
Hide the wet stall, long absent from the sea;
And where the cleaver chops the heifer's spoil;
And where huge hogsheads sweat with trainy oil,
Thy breathing nostril hold: but how shall I
Pass where, in piles, Cornavion[3] cheeses lie?
Cheese, that the table's closing rites denies,
And bids me with the unwilling chaplain rise.
  O bear me to the paths of fair Pall Mall:
Safe are thy pavements, grateful is thy smell!
At distance rolls along the gilded coach,
Nor sturdy carmen on thy walks encroach;
No lets would bar thy ways, were chairs denied,
The soft supports of laziness and pride; [glow,
Shops breathe perfumes, through sashes ribbons
The mutual arms of ladies and the beau:
Yet still ev'n here, when rains the passage hide,
Oft the loose stone spirts up a muddy tide
Beneath thy careless foot; and from on high,
Where masons mount the ladder, fragments fly;
Mortar and crumbled lime in showers descend,
And o'er thy head destructive tiles impend.
  But sometimes let me leave the noisy roads,
And silent wander in the close abodes, [sive stray,
Where wheels ne'er shake the ground; there pen-
In studious thought, the long uncrowded way.

[2] Thames Street. [3] Cheshire, anciently so called.

Here I remark each walker's different face,
And in their look their various business trace.
The broker here his spacious beaver wears,
Upon his brow sit jealousies and cares;
Bent on some mortgage (to avoid reproach)
He seeks by-streets, and saves the expensive coach.
Soft, at low doors, old lechers tap their cane,
For fair recluse, who travels Drury-lane;
Here roams uncomb'd the lavish rake, to shun
His Fleet-street draper's everlasting dun.
Careful observers, studious of the Town,
Shun the misfortunes that disgrace the clown;
Untempted, they contemn the juggler's feats,
Pass'd by the Muse, nor try the thimble's cheats.[4]
When drays bound high, they never cross behind,
Where bubbling yest is blown by gusts of wind:
And when up Ludgate-hill huge carts move slow,
Far from the straining steeds securely go,
Whose dashing hoofs behind them fling the mire,
And mark with muddy blots the gazing 'squire.
The Parthian thus his javelin backward throws,
And as he flies infests pursuing foes.
The thoughtless wits shall frequent forfeits pay,
Who 'gainst the sentry's box discharge their tea:
Do thou some court or secret corner seek,
Nor flush with shame the passing virgin's cheek.

[4] A cheat commonly practised with three thimbles and a little ball.

Yet let me not descend to trivial song,
Nor vulgar circumstance my verse prolong.
Why should I teach the maid, when torrents pour,
Her head to shelter from the sudden shower?
Nature will best her ready hand inform,
With her spread petticoat to fence the storm.
Does not each walker know the warning sign,
When wisps of straw depend upon the twine
Cross the close street, that then the paver's art
Renews the ways, denied to coach and cart?
Who knows not that the coachman lashing by,
Oft with his flourish cuts the heedless eye?
And when he takes his stand, to wait a fare,
His horses' foreheads shun the winter's air?
Nor will I roam when summer's sultry rays
Parch the dry ground, and spread with dust the ways;
With whirling gusts the rapid atoms rise,
Smoke o'er the pavement, and involve the skies.

Winter my theme confines, whose nitry wind
Shall crust the slabby mire, and kennels bind;
She bids the snow descend in flaky sheets,
And in her hoary mantle clothe the streets.
Let not the virgin tread these slippery roads,
The gathering fleece the hollow patten loads;
But if thy footsteps slide with clotted frost,
Strike off the breaking balls against the post.
On silent wheel the passing coaches roll,
Oft look behind and ward the threatening pole.

In harden'd orbs the schoolboy moulds the snow,
To mark the coachman with a dexterous throw.
Why do ye, boys! the kennel's surface spread,
To tempt with faithless pass the matron's tread?
How can ye laugh to see the damsel spurn,
Sink in your frauds, and her green stocking mourn?
At White's the harness'd chairman idly stands,
And swings around his waist his tingling hands:
The sempstress speeds to Change with red-tipt nose,
The Belgian stove beneath her footstool glows:
In half-whipt muslin needles useless lie,
And shuttle-cocks across the counter fly.
These sports warm harmless; why then will ye prove,
Deluded maids! the dangerous flame of love?
Where Covent-Garden's famous temple stands,
That boasts the work of Jones' immortal hands,
Columns with plain magnificence appear,
And graceful porches lead along the square;
Here oft my course I bend, when, lo! from far
I spy the furies of the foot-ball war:
The 'prentice quits his shop to join the crew,
Increasing crowds the flying game pursue.
Thus, as you roll the ball o'er snowy ground,
The gathering globe augments with every round.
But whither shall I run? the throng draws nigh;
The ball now skims the street, now soars on high;
The dextrous glazier strong returns the bound,
And jingling sashes on the penthouse sound.

O roving Muse! recall that wondrous year
When winter reign'd in bleak Britannia's air;
When hoary Thames, with frosted osiers crown'd,
Was three long moons in icy fetters bound.
The waterman, forlorn along the shore,
Pensive reclines upon his useless oar,
Sees harness'd steeds desert the stony Town,
And wander roads unstable, not their own;
Wheels o'er the harden'd waters smoothly glide,
And rase with whiten'd tracks the slippery tide.
Here the fat cook piles high the blazing fire,
And scarce the spit can turn the steer entire.
Booths sudden hide the Thames, long streets appear,
And numerous games proclaim the crowded fair.
So when a general bids the martial train
Spread their encampment o'er the spacious plain,
Thick rising tents a canvas city build,
And the loud dice resound through all the field.
'Twas here the matron found a doleful fate;
Let elegiac lay the woe relate,
Soft as the breath of distant flutes at hours
When silent evening closes up the flowers,
Lulling as falling water's hollow noise,
Indulging grief, like Philomela's voice.
Doll every day had walk'd these treacherous roads,
Her neck grew warpt beneath autumnal loads
Of various fruit; she now a basket bore:
That head, alas! shall basket bear no more.

Each booth she frequent past in quest of gain,
And boys with pleasure heard her shrilling strain.
Ah! Doll! all mortals must resign their breath,
And industry itself submit to death.
The cracking crystal yields; she sinks, she dies;
Her head, chopt off, from her lost shoulders flies:
Pippins she cry'd, but death her voice confounds,
And pip,-pip,-pip, along the ice resounds.
So when the Thracian furies Orpheus tore,
And left his bleeding trunk deform'd with gore,
His sever'd head floats down the silver tide,
His yet warm tongue for his lost consort cried;
Eurydice with quivering voice he mourn'd,
And Heber's banks Eurydice return'd.
But now the western gale the flood unbinds,
And blackening clouds move on with warmer winds,
The wooden town its frail foundation leaves,
And Thames' full urn rolls down his plenteous waves;
From every penthouse streams the fleeting snow,
And with dissolving frost the pavements flow.
Experienc'd men, inur'd to city ways,
Need not the calendar to count their days.
When through the Town, with slow and solemn air,
Led by the nostril, walks the muzzled bear,
Behind him moves majestically dull,
The pride of Hockley-hole, the surly bull;
Learn hence the periods of the week to name:
Mondays and Thursdays are the days of game.

When fishy stalls with double store are laid,
The golden-bellied carp, the broad-finn'd maid,
Red-speckled trouts, the salmon's silver jowl,
The jointed lobster, and unscaly sole,
And luscious 'scallops to allure the tastes
Of rigid zealots to delicious fasts;
Wednesdays and Fridays, you 'll observe from hence,
Days when our sires were doom'd to abstinence.
When dirty waters from balconies drop,
And dextrous damsels twirl the sprinkling mop,
And cleanse the spatter'd sash, and scrub the stairs,
Know Saturday's conclusive morn appears.
Successive cries the seasons' change declare,
And mark the monthly progress of the year.
Hark! how the streets with treble voices ring,
To sell the bounteous product of the spring:
Sweet-smelling flowers, and elder's early bud,
With nettle's tender shoots, to cleanse the blood:
And when June's thunder cools the sultry skies,
Ev'n Sundays are profan'd by mackrel cries.
Walnuts the fruiterer's hand, in autumn, stain,
Blue plums and juicy pears augment his gain;
Next oranges the longing boys entice
To trust their copper fortunes to the dice.
When rosemary, and bays, the poet's crown,
Are bawl'd in frequent cries through all the Town,
Then judge the festival of Christmas near,
Christmas! the joyous period of the year.
Now with bright holly all your temples strow,
With laurel green, and sacred misletoe:

Now, heav'n-born Charity! thy blessings shed,
Bid meagre Want upear her sickly head:
Bid shivering limbs be warm; let Plenty's bowl
In humble roofs make glad the needy soul.
See, see! the heav'n-born maid her blessings shed;
Lo! meagre Want uprears her sickly head;
Cloth'd are the naked, and the needy glad,
While selfish Avarice alone is sad.

Proud coaches pass, regardless of the moan
Of infant orphan's and the widow's groan,
While charity still moves the walker's mind,
His liberal purse relieves the lame and blind.
Judiciously thy halfpence are bestow'd,
Where the laborious beggar sweeps the road.
Whate'er you give, give ever at demand,
Nor let old age long stretch his palsied hand.
Those who give late are importun'd each day,
And still are teas'd because they still delay.
If e'er the miser durst his farthings spare,
He thinly spreads them through the public square,
Where, all beside the rail, rang'd beggars lie,
And from each other catch the doleful cry; [score,
With Heav'n, for two-pence, cheaply wipes his
Lifts up his eyes, and hastes to beggar more.

Where the brass knocker, wrapt in flannel band,
Forbids the thunder of the footman's hand,
The upholder, rueful harbinger of death,
Waits with impatience for the dying breath;
As vultures o'er a camp, with hovering flight,
Snuff up the future carnage of the fight.

Here canst thou pass unmindful of a prayer,
That Heav'n in mercy may thy brother spare?
  Come, F * * * ! sincere, experienc'd friend,
Thy briefs, thy deeds, and ev'n thy fees, suspend;
Come, let us leave the Temple's silent walls,
Me business to my distant lodging calls:
Through the long Strand together let us stray;
With thee conversing I forget the way.
Behold that narrow street which steep descends,
Whose building to the slimy shore extends;
Here Arundel's fam'd structure rear'd its frame,
The street alone retains an empty name.
Where Titian's glowing paint the canvas warm'd,
And Raphael's fair design with judgment charm'd,
Now hangs the bellman's song, and pasted here
The colour'd prints of Overton appear.
Where statues breath'd the works of Phidias' hands,
A wooden pump or lonely watch-house stands.
There Essex' stately pile adorn'd the shore,
There Cecils', Bedfords' Villiers', now no more.
Yet Burlington's fair palace still remains;
Beauty within, without proportion reigns.
Beneath his eye declining Art revives,
The wall with animated picture lives.
There Handel strikes the strings, the melting strain
Transports the soul, and thrills through every vein.
There oft I enter (but with cleaner shoes)
For Burlington's belov'd by every Muse.

O ye associate walkers! O my friends!
Upon your state what happiness attends!
What though no coach to frequent visit rolls,
Nor, for your shilling, chairmen sling their poles?
Yet still your nerves rheumatic pains defy,
Nor lazy jaundice dulls your saffron eye;
No wasting cough discharges sounds of death,
Nor wheezing asthma heaves in vain for breath;
Nor from your restless couch is heard the groan
Of burning gout or sedentary stone.
Let others in the jolting coach confide,
Or in the leaky boat the Thames divide;
Or, box'd within the chair, contemn the street,
And trust their safety to another's feet:
Still let me walk; for oft the sudden gale
Ruffles the tide, and shifts the dangerous sail:
Then shall the passenger too late deplore
The whelming billow and the faithless oar;
The drunken chairman in the kennel spurns,
The glasses shatters, and his charge o'erturns.
Who can recount the coach's various harms,
The legs disjointed, and the broken arms?
I've seen a beau, in some ill-fated hour,
When o'er the stones chok'd kennels swell the shower,
In gilded chariot loll; he with disdain
Views spatter'd passengers all drench'd in rain.
With mud fill'd high, the rumbling cart draws near;
Now rule thy prancing steeds, lac'd charioteer;

The dustman lashes on with spiteful rage,
His pondrous spokes thy painted wheel engage;
Crush'd is thy pride, down falls the shrieking beau,
The slabby pavement crystal fragments strow;
Black floods of mire the embroider'd coat disgrace,
And mud enwraps the honours of his face:—
So when dread Jove the son of Phœbus hurl'd,
Scar'd with dark thunder, to the nether world,
The headstrong coursers tore the silver reins,
And the sun's beamy ruin gilds the plains.
  If the pale walker pant with weakening ills,
His sickly hand is stor'd with friendly bills:
From hence he learns the seventh-born doctor's fame;
From hence he learns the cheapest tailor's name.
  Shall the large mutton smoke upon your boards?
Such Newgate's copious market best affords.
Wouldst thou with mighty beef augment thy meal?
Seek Leaden-hall: St James's sends thee veal;
Thames-street gives cheeses; Covent-garden, fruits;
Moor-fields, old books; and Monmouth-street, old suits.
Hence may'st thou well supply the wants of life,
Support thy family, and clothe thy wife.
  Volumes on shelter'd stalls expanded lie,
And various science lures the learned eye;

The bending shelves with pondrous scholiasts groan,
And deep divines, to modern shops unknown:
Here, like the bee, that on industrious wing
Collects the various odours of the spring,
Walkers, at leisure, Learning's flowers may spoil,
Nor watch the wasting of the midnight oil;
May morals snatch from Plutarch's tatter'd page,
A mildew'd Bacon, or Stagira's sage:
Here sauntering 'prentices o'er Otway weep,
O'er Congreve smile, or over Durfy sleep:
Pleas'd sempstresses the Lock's fam'd Rape unfold,
And Squirts [5] read Garth, 'till apozems grow cold.
O Lintot! let my labours obvious lie,
Rang'd on thy stall, for every curious eye;
So shall the poor these precepts gratis know,
And to my verse their future safeties owe.
What walker shall his mean ambition fix
On the false lustre of a coach and six?
Let the vain virgin, lur'd by glaring show,
Sigh for the liveries of the embroider'd beau.
See yon bright chariot on its harness swing,
With Flanders mares, and on an arched spring:
That wretch, to gain an equipage and place,
Betray'd his sister to a lewd embrace.

[5] The name of an apothecary's boy, in the Poem of 'The Dispensary.'

This coach that with the blazon'd 'scutcheon glows,
Vain of his unknown race, the coxcomb shows.
Here the brib'd lawyer, sunk in velvet, sleeps;
The starving orphan, as he passes, weeps:
There flames a fool, begirt with tinsell'd slaves,
Who wastes the wealth of a whole race of knaves.
That other, with a clustering train behind,
Owes his new honours to a sordid mind.
This next in court-fidelity excels,
The public rifles, and his country sells.
May the proud chariot never be my fate,
If purchas'd at so mean, so dear a rate:
Or rather give me sweet content on foot,
Wrapt in my virtue and a good surtout!

BOOK III.

OF WALKING THE STREETS BY NIGHT.

O Trivia! goddess, leave these low abodes,
And traverse o'er the wide ethereal roads;
Celestial queen! put on thy robes of light,
Now Cynthia nam'd, fair regent of the night.
At sight of thee the villain sheathes his sword,
Nor scales the wall, to steal the wealthy hoard.
O may thy silver lamp from Heaven's high bower
Direct my footsteps in the midnight hour!
When night first bids the twinkling stars appear,
Or with her cloudy vest inwraps the air,
Then swarms the busy street: with caution tread
Where the shop-windows falling threat thy head:
Now labourers home return, and join their strength
To bear the tottering plank or ladder's length;
Still fix thy eyes intent upon the throng,
And as the passes open, wind along.
Where the fair columns of Saint Clement stand,
Whose straiten'd bounds encroach upon the Strand;
Where the low penthouse bows the walker's head,
And the rough pavement wounds the yielding tread;

Where not a post protects the narrow space,
And, strung in twines, combs dangle in thy face;
Summon at once thy courage, rouse thy care,
Stand firm, look back, be resolute, beware:
Forth issuing from steep lanes, the collier's steeds
Drag the black load; another cart succeeds;
Team follows team, crowds heap'd on crowds appear,
And wait impatient till the road grow clear.
Now all the pavement sounds with trampling feet,
And the mixt hurry barricades the street.
Entangled here, the wagon's lengthen'd team
Cracks the tough harness; here a pondrous beam
Lies overturn'd athwart; for slaughter fed,
Here lowing bullocks raise their horned head.
Now oaths grow loud, with coaches coaches jar,
And the smart blow provokes the sturdy war:
From the high box they whirl the thong around,
And with the twining lash their shins resound:
Their rage ferments, more dangerous wounds they try,
And the blood gushes down their painful eye.
And now on foot the frowning warriors light,
And with their pondrous fists renew the fight;
Blow answers blow, their cheeks are smear'd with blood,
Till down they fall, and grappling roll in mud.
So when two boars, in wild Ytene[1] bred,
Or on Westphalia's fattening chestnuts fed,

[1] New Forest in Hampshire, anciently so called.

Gnash their sharp tusks, and, rous'd with equal fire,
Dispute the reign of some luxurious mire;
In the black flood they wallow o'er and o'er,
Till their arm'd jaws distil with foam and gore.
  Where the mob gathers, swiftly shoot along,
Nor idly mingle in the noisy throng.
Lur'd by the silver hilt, amid the swarm
The subtle artist will thy side disarm:
Nor is thy flaxen wig with safety worn;
High on the shoulder in a basket borne
Lurks the sly boy, whose hand, to rapine bred,
Plucks off the curling honours of thy head.
Here dives the skulking thief, with practis'd sleight
And unfelt fingers makes thy pocket light.
Where's now thy watch? with all its trinkets, flown;
And thy late snuff-box is no more thy own.
But, lo! his bolder thefts some tradesman spies,
Swift from his prey the scudding lurcher flies:
Dextrous he 'scapes the coach with nimble bounds,
Whilst every honest tongue 'Stop thief' resounds.
So speeds the wily fox, alarm'd by fear,
Who lately filch'd the turkey's callow care;
Hounds following hounds, grow louder as he flies,
And injur'd tenants join the hunter's cries:
Breathless he stumbling falls. Ill-fated boy!
Why did not honest work thy youth employ?
Seiz'd by rough hands, he's dragg'd amid the rout,
And stretch'd beneath the pump's incessant spout;

Or plung'd in miry pounds he gasping lies,
Mud choaks his mouth, and plasters o'er his eyes.
  Let not the ballad-singer's shrilling strain
Amid the swarm thy listening ear detain;
Guard well thy pocket; for these sirens stand
To aid the labours of the diving hand:
Confederate in the cheat, they draw the throng,
And cambric handkerchiefs reward the song.
But soon as coach or cart drives rattling on,
The rabble part, in shoals they backward run:
So Jove's loud bolts the mingled war divide,
And Greece and Troy retreat on either side.
  If the rude throng pour on with furious pace,
And hap to break thee from a friend's embrace,
Stop short; nor struggle through the crowd in vain,
But watch with careful eye the passing train.
Yet I (perhaps too fond) if chance the tide,
Tumultuous, bear my partner from my side,
Impatient venture back; despising harm,
I force my passage where the thickest swarm.
Thus his lost bride the Trojan sought in vain
Through night, and arms, and flames, and hills of slain:
Thus Nisus wander'd o'er the pathless grove,
To find the brave companion of his love:
The pathless grove in vain he wanders o'er:
Euryalus, alas! is now no more.
  That walker who, regardless of his pace,
Turns oft to pore upon the damsel's face,

From side to side by thrusting elbows tost,
Shall strike his aching breast against a post;
Or water, dash'd from fishy stalls, shall stain
His hapless coat with spirts of scaly rain.
But if unwarily he chance to stray,
Where twirling turnstiles intercept the way;
The thwarting passenger shall force them round,
And beat the wretch half breathless to the ground.
Let constant vigilance thy footsteps guide,
And wary circumspection guard thy side;
Then shalt thou walk unharm'd the dangerous night,
Nor need the officious linkboy's smoky light.
Thou never wilt attempt to cross the road
Where alehouse benches rest the porter's load,
Grievous to heedless shins; no barrow's wheel,
That bruises oft the truant schoolboy's heel,
Behind thee rolling, with insidious pace,
Shall mark thy stocking with a miry trace.
Let not thy venturous steps approach too nigh
Where, gaping wide, low steepy cellars lie;
Should thy shoe wrench aside, down, down you fall,
And overturn the scolding huckster's stall;
The scolding huckster shall not o'er thee moan,
But pence exact for nuts and pears o'erthrown.
Though you through cleanlier alleys wind by day,
To shun the hurries of the public way,
Yet ne'er to those dark paths by night retire;
Mind only safety, and contemn the mire.

Then no impervious courts thy haste detain,
Nor sneering alewives bid thee turn again.
Where Lincoln's-Inn, wide space, is rail'd around,
Cross not with venturous step; there oft is found
The lurking thief, who, while the daylight shone,
Made the walls echo with his begging tone:
That crutch, which late compassion mov'd, shall wound
Thy bleeding head, and fell thee to the ground.
Though thou art tempted by the linkman's call,
Yet trust him not along the lonely wall;
In the mid-way he 'll quench the flaming brand,
And share the booty with the pilfering band.
Still keep the public streets, where oily rays,
Shot from the crystal lamp, o'erspread the ways.
Happy Augusta! law-defended town!
Here no dark lanterns shade the villain's frown:
No Spanish jealousies thy lanes infest,
Nor Roman vengeance stabs the unwary breast;
Here Tyranny ne'er lifts her purple hand,
But Liberty and Justice guard the land:
No bravos here profess the bloody trade,
Nor is the church the murderer's refuge made.
Let not the chairman, with assuming stride,
Press near the wall, and rudely thrust thy side:
The laws have set him bounds; his servile feet
Should ne'er encroach where posts defend the street.

Yet who the footman's arrogance can quell,
Whose flambeau gilds the sashes of Pall-Mall,
When in long rank a train of torches flame,
To light the midnight visits of the dame?
Others, perhaps, by happier guidance led,
May where the chairman rests with safety tread:
Whene'er I pass, their poles unseen below,
Make my knee tremble with the jarring blow.
  If wheels bar up the road where streets are crost,
With gentle words the coachman's ear accost:
He ne'er the threat or harsh command obeys,
But with contempt the spatter'd shoe surveys.
Now, man with utmost fortitude thy soul,
To cross the way where carts and coaches roll;
Yet do not in thy hardy skill confide,
Nor rashly risk the kennel's spacious stride:
Stay till *afar* the distant wheel you hear,
Like dying thunder in the breaking air:
Thy foot will slide upon the miry stone,
And passing coaches crush thy tortur'd bone,
Or wheels enclose the road; on either hand,
Pent round with perils, in the midst you stand,
And call for aid in vain; the coachman swears;
And carmen drive, unmindful of thy prayers.
Where wilt thou turn? ah! whither wilt thou fly?
On every side the pressing spokes are nigh:
So sailors, while Charybdis' gulf they shun,
Amaz'd, on Scylla's craggy dangers run.

Be sure observe where brown Ostrea stands,
Who boasts her shelly ware from Wallfleet sands;
There may'st thou pass, with safe unmiry feet,
Where the rais'd pavement leads athwart the street.
If where Fleet-ditch with muddy current flows
You chance to roam; where oyster tubs in rows
Are rang'd beside the posts; there stay thy haste,
And with the savoury fish indulge thy taste:
The damsel's knife the gaping shell commands,
While the salt liquor streams between her hands.
The man had sure a palate cover'd o'er
With brass or steel, that on the rocky shore
First broke the oozy oyster's pearly coat,
And risk'd the living morsel down his throat.
What will not luxury taste? Earth, sea, and air,
Are daily ransack'd for the bill of fare.
Blood stuff'd in skins is British Christian's food,
And France robs marshes of the croaking brood;
Spongy morels in strong ragouts are found,
And in the soup the slimy snail is drown'd.
When from high spouts the dashing torrents fall,
Ever be watchful to maintain the wall;
For shouldst thou quit thy ground, the rushing throng
Will with impetuous fury drive along;
All press to gain those honours thou hast lost,
And rudely shove thee far without the post.
Then to retrieve the shed you strive in vain,
Draggled all o'er, and soak'd in floods of rain.

Yet rather bear the shower, and toils of mud,
Than in the doubtful quarrel risk thy blood.
O think on Œdipus' detested state,
And by his woes be warn'd to shun thy fate.
Where three roads join'd he met his sire unknown,
(Unhappy sire, but more unhappy son!)
Each claim'd the way; their swords the strife decide;
The hoary monarch fell; he groan'd and died!
Hence sprung the fatal plague that thinn'd thy reign,
Thy cursed incest! and thy children slain!
Hence wert thou doom'd in endless night to stray
Through Theban streets, and cheerless grope thy way.
Contemplate, mortal! on thy fleeting years;
See, with black train the funeral pomp appears!
Whether some heir attends in sable state,
And mourns with outward grief a parent's fate,
Or the fair virgin, nipt in beauty's bloom,
A crowd of lovers follow to her tomb;
Why is the hearse with scutcheons blazon'd round,
And with the nodding plume of ostrich crown'd?
No; the dead know it not, nor profit gain;
It only serves to prove the living, vain.
How short is life! how frail is human trust!
Is all this pomp for laying dust to dust?
Where the nail'd hoop defends the painted stall,
Brush not thy sweeping skirt too near the wall;

Thy heedless sleeve will drink the colour'd oil,
And spot indelible thy pocket soil.
Has not wise Nature strung the legs and feet
With firmest nerves, designed to walk the street?
Has she not given us hands to grope aright,
Amidst the frequent dangers of the night?
And think'st thou not the double nostril meant
To warn from oily woes by previous scent?
  Who can the various city frauds recite,
With all the petty rapines of the night?
Who now the guinea-dropper's bait regards,
Trick'd by the sharper's dice or juggler's cards?
Why should I warn thee ne'er to join the fray
Where the sham-quarrel interrupts the way?
Lives there in these our days so soft a clown,
Braved by the bully's oaths or threatening frown?
I need not strict enjoin the pockets care,
When from the crowded play thou lead'st the fair;
Who has not here or watch or snuff-box lost,
Or handkerchiefs that India's shuttle boast;
O! may thy virtue guard thee through the roads
Of Drury's mazy courts and dark abodes,
The harlots' guileful paths, who nightly stand
Where Catherine-street descends into the Strand.
Say, vagrant Muse! their wiles and subtle arts,
To lure the strangers' unsuspecting hearts;
So shall our youth on healthful sinews tread,
And city cheeks grow warm with rural red.
  'Tis she who nightly strolls with sauntering pace,
No stubborn stays her yielding shape embrace;

Beneath the lamp her tawdry ribbons glare,
The new-scour'd mantua and the slattern air;
High-draggled petticoats her travels show,
And hollow cheeks with artful blushes glow;
With flattering sounds she soothes the cred'lous ear,
My noble captain! charmer! love! my dear!
In ridinghood near tavern-doors she plies,
Or muffled pinners hide her livid eyes;
With empty bandbox she delights to range,
And feigns a distant errand from the 'Change;
Nay, she will oft the quaker's hood profane,
And trudge demure the rounds of Drury-lane:
She darts from sarcenet ambush wily leers;
Twitches thy sleeve, or with familiar airs
Her fan will pat thy cheek: these snares disdain,
Nor gaze behind thee when she turns again.
  I knew a yeoman who for thirst of gain,
To the great city drove from Devon's plain,
His numerous lowing herd: his herds he sold,
And his deep leathern pocket bagg'd with gold:
Drawn by a fraudful nymph, he gaz'd, he sighed;
Unmindful of his home, and distant bride,
She leads the willing victim to his doom,
Through winding alleys to her cobweb room.
Thence through the street he reels, from post to post,
Valiant with wine, nor knows his treasure lost.
The vagrant wretch the assembled watchman spies,
He waves his hanger and their poles defies;

Deep in the roundhouse pent, all night he snores,
And the next morn in vain his fate deplores.
  Ah! hapless swain! unus'd to pains and ills,
Canst thou forego roast beef for nauseous pills?
How wilt thou lift to heaven thy eyes and hands,
When the long scroll the surgeon's fees demands!
Or else (ye gods! avert that worst disgrace)
Thy ruin'd nose falls level with thy face;
Then shall thy wife thy loathsome kiss disdain,
And wholesome neighbours from thy mug refrain.
  Yet there are watchmen who, with friendly light
Will teach thy reeling steps to tread aright;
For sixpence will support thy helpless arm,
And home conduct thee safe from nightly harm;
But if they shake their lanterns, from afar
To call their brethren to confederate war,
When rakes resist their power; if hapless you
Should chance to wander with the scouring crew!
Though Fortune yield thee captive, ne'er despair,
But seek the constable's considerate ear;
He will reverse the watchman's harsh decree,
Mov'd by the rhetoric of a silver fee.
Thus would you gain some favourite courtier's word,
Fee not the petty clerks, but bribe my lord.
  Now is the time that rakes their revels keep,
Kindlers of riot, enemies of sleep.
His scatter'd pence the flying Nicker[2] flings,
And with the copper shower the casement rings.

2 Gentlemen who delighted to break windows with half pence.

Who has not heard the scourer's midnight fame?
Who has not trembled at the Mohock's name?
Was there a watchman took his hourly rounds
Safe from their blows, or new-invented wounds?
I pass their desperate deeds and mischiefs done,
Where from Snow-hill black steepy torrents run;
How matrons, hoop'd within the hogshead's womb,
Were tumbled furious thence; the rolling tomb
O'er the stones thunders, bounds from side to side;
So Regulus to save his country died.

Where a dim gleam the paly lantern throws
O'er the mid pavement, heapy rubbish grows;
Or arched vaults their gaping jaws extend,
Or the dark caves to common sewers descend;
Oft by the winds extinct the signal lies,
Or smother'd in the glimmering socket dies,
Ere Night has half roll'd round her ebon throne,
In the wide gulf the shatter'd coach o'erthrown
Sinks with the snorting steeds; the reins are broke,
And from the crackling axle flies the spoke.
So when fam'd Eddystone's far-shoooting ray,
That led the sailor through the stormy way,
Was from its rocky roots by billows torn,
And the high turret in the whirlwind borne,
Fleets bulg'd their sides against the craggy land,
And pitchy ruins blacken'd all the strand.

Who then through night would hire the harness'd steed?
And who would choose the rattling wheel for speed?

But hark! distress with screaming voice draws nigher.
And wakes the slumbering street with cries of 'fire!'
At first a glowing red enwraps the skies,
And borne by winds the scattering sparks arise;
From beam to beam the fierce contagion spreads;
The spiry flames now lift aloft their heads;
Through the burst sash a blazing deluge pours,
And splitting tiles descend in rattling showers.
Now with thick crowds the enlighten'd pavement swarms,
The fireman sweats beneath his crooked arms;
A leathern casque his venturous head defends,
Boldly he climbs where thickest smoke ascends;
Mov'd by the mother's streaming eyes and prayers,
The hepless infant through the flame he bears,
With no less virtue than through hostile fire
The Dardan hero bore his aged sire.
See forceful engines spout their levell'd streams,
To quench the blaze that runs along the beams;
The grappling hook plucks rafters from the walls,
And heaps on heaps the smoky ruin falls.
Blown by strong winds, the fiery tempest roars,
Bears down new walls, and pours along the floors;
The heavens are all a-blaze, the face of night
Is cover'd with a sanguine dreadful light;
'Twas such a light involv'd thy towers, O Rome!
The dire presage of mighty Cæsar's doom,
When the sun veil'd in rust his mourning head,
And frightful prodigies the skies o'erspread.

Hark! the drum thunders! far, ye crowds! retire:
Behold! the ready match is tipt with fire,
The nitrous store is laid, the smutty train
With running blaze awakes the barrell'd grain;
Flames sudden wrap the walls; with sullen sound
The shatter'd pile sinks on the smoky ground.
So when the years shall have revolv'd the date,
The inevitable hour of Naples' fate,
Her sapp'd foundations shall with thunders shake,
And heave and toss upon the sulphurous lake;
Earth's womb at once the fiery flood shall rend,
And in the abyss her plunging towers descend.
Consider, reader! what fatigues I've known,
The toils, the perils of the wintry town;
What riots seen, what bustling crowds I bor'd,
How oft I cross'd where carts and coaches roar'd:
Yet shall I bless my labours, if mankind
Their future safety from my dangers find.
Thus the bold traveller, (inur'd to toil,
Whose steps have printed Asia's desert soil,
The barbarous Arabs' haunt, or shivering crost
Dark Greenland's mountains of eternal frost,
Whom Providence in length of years restores
To the wish'd harbour of his native shores)
Sets forth his journals to the public view,
To caution, by his woes, the wandering crew.
And now complete my generous labours lie,
Finish'd, and ripe for immortality.
Death shall entomb in dust this mouldering frame,
But never reach the eternal part, my fame.

When W* and G**, mighty Names! are dead,
Or but a Chelsea, under custards, read;
When critics crazy bandboxes repair,
And tragedies, turn'd rockets, bounce in air,
High-rais'd on Fleet-street posts, consign'd to fame,
This work shall shine, and walkers bless my name.

INDEX.

END OF VOL. I.

www.ingramcontent.com/pod-product-compliance
Lightning Source LLC
LaVergne TN
LVHW010215110826
845151LV00004B/1087

* 9 7 8 1 4 2 5 5 2 8 1 1 9 *